T0199155

EFFECTIVE CHURCH PLANTING

A Primer for Establishing New Testament Churches in the New Millennium

DR. J HERNES ABANTE

WESTBOW
PRESS®
A DIVISION OF THOMAS NELSON
& ZONDERVAN

WestBow Press books may be ordered through booksellers or by contacting:

WestBow Press
A Division of Thomas Nelson & Zondervan
1663 Liberty Drive
Bloomington, IN 47403
www.westbowpress.com
1 (866) 928-1240

ISBN: 978-1-5127-5808-5 (sc)
ISBN: 978-1-5127-5809-2 (hc)
ISBN: 978-1-5127-5807-8 (e)

Library of Congress Control Number: 2016915859

Print information available on the last page.

WestBow Press rev. date: 09/22/2016

In loving memory of my dear father,

Dr. Ben O. Abante Sr.

He was also my friend, mentor, and brother in the Lord. His life and example have served as my daily inspiration.

His strong conviction regarding the local New Testament church and uncompromised stand on the doctrine of Baptist distinctives made this primer possible.

CONTENTS

ACKNOWLEDGMENTS

I wish to express my deepest gratitude to Bishop Reuben Abante, senior pastor of the Lighthouse Bible Baptist Church and member of the Presidential Council on Values Formation in the Philippines, who has generously shared his office and resources in the formation of this book. I also wish to thank Joaquin "Jake" Santiago, for his invaluable help in the final editing and formatting of this book; Hannah Hazel Morales and John William Morales, the sister and brother team who helped in the formatting, editing, and design; Bootes Esden-Lopos, for helping in the final editing and proofreading; Mercy Corrales Santiago, Helen Grace Abante, and Agatha Tapan, for helping in the initial editing; my brother, Congressman Benny Abante Jr; my daughter, Naomi Abante Thesius; and my dear wife, Angelita Falcone Abante, for their encouragement and understanding during the writing of this book. I also wish to thank my God and Savior, the Lord Jesus Christ, the founder of the New Testament church and other churches of like faith and practice.

To Him be all the glory!

PREFACE

This primer took years to develop, obviously not in its writing but in the accumulation of the wealth of knowledge contained here. The information in this book covers the vast observations I have personally witnessed and experienced as a young child growing up in a Christian home, as an impressionistic teenager, as an ambitious young man, as an idealistic husband and father (though not an ideal one), and lastly as a man of God with a desire to please only Him. This is a book about church ministry and the works and calling of a God-called man, the preacher.

Although this is my own writing, the real authors are those people who have made great impressions on my life. They include my parents; my brothers, who are both pastors of successful churches in the Philippines; my teachers and mentors here and abroad; coworkers in the churches where I labored; seminary classmates; friends; and others who in one way or another have made an impact on my life with their dedication to serve God. They have all contributed to my understanding of the work of the Lord. God has used them greatly in my ministry.

Writing has never been my cup of tea. I've always described myself as a "trying-hard writer." However, I take pride in having a high regard of reading on various subjects, such that I have collected volumes of books that have left deep impressions on my life. My focus in reading is simply to study how people interact with others and how they observe their environment. It always excites and intrigues me to know how authors look at life. Their views on life pique my excitement and intrigue not so much because of what these authors say but more on how he or she state his or her views. This isn't about the information per se (although that is important) but about how the author perceives and applies it in his or her everyday life. This is about how the wealth of information impacts him or her and others.

My exposure to different volumes of books led me to regard the one book, the word of God, as being far above and different from any other book. I find it more powerful and appealing because of how it has helped man throughout the centuries. The status of this book is incomparable with others. Time isn't wasted when one reads this great book. It contains the mind of God. It has become my inspiration, and by it I find myself scrutinizing other literature in light of what the Bible declares.

Because of this, I started writing to describe my observations through the years and hopefully to help others in experiencing the power of the word of God as it is being applied in life. My prayer and hope are that this primer will serve the purpose of sharing with you how God has influenced my life and how He has used me for His honor and glory. I want to declare how God works in the hearts of men and show the relevance of the truths He has given in His word.

This primer contains the truths that have been tried by and passed the tests of time. Consider these principles as you sift through the pages of this primer. As you do, pray for wisdom and understanding. Whatever reasons you might have in acquiring or reading this book, I trust that you take the nuggets found here and apply them in your life. My desire is that these principles would be shared with others, especially with those having a desire to serve the Lord in the ministry of church planting.

My Mother's Love

Dedicated to my mother, Priscilla M. Abante, and to those ravaged with amyotrophic lateral sclerosis (ALS) more commonly known as Lou Gehrig's disease.

She lies, longing to leave, but her eyes
Wish to express that she loves us.
Her frail body confines a soul still beaming
With faith that has moved mountains,
Crossed deep valleys and boiling streams.
She never gives up, not an utter of complaint.
Her inward strength continues to radiate
Through her weak, fragile body, reaching out
With her withered fingers to touch.

I could hear her thoughts, her silent cries,
Her laughter from memories past.
Her warm, tender lips on my forehead and
The spread of cotton to warm me at night
Are still vividly fresh in my mind.
Her singing, sighing, and the clap of her
Hands to praise echo in my ears.
Soon she will leave us but linger, and
ALS will be gone forever in the blue sky.

—Hernes M. Abante

INTRODUCTION

The New Testament church is an institution the Lord Jesus Christ started during His personal earthly ministry. It is an organism capable of growth and action. Like the first institution He established, the family, He expects the church to grow, propagate, and multiply. This is spiritual procreation and perpetuation. God intends for His church, composed of people He has called unto salvation and obedience to scriptural baptism and instruction, to come together and be part of this local assembly—the spiritual family—to fulfill the mission of reaching the world with the good news of the gospel. This assembly has to continue building, expanding, growing, and perpetuating until the coming back of the founder, the Lord Jesus Christ.

The biblical idea of a church is local and visible. It is neither the universal visible church of the Roman Catholic persuasion nor the universal invisible church of the Protestant movement. Neither does it refer to any organized religion men started throughout the ages. It has no semblance to any denominational organizations or any similar groups that claim to have the mandate of God. You find these groups all over the world, trying to take the place of the true church, the New Testament assembly. There is no way they can fit the description of what Jesus organized. No way can they be identified with it unless they can trace their history and authority back to the Jerusalem church.

The church, or "ecclesia" in its Greek form, refers to the people God has personally called unto salvation. They are obedient to the commandment of scriptural baptism and united to fulfill the commission found in Matthew 28:19–20. The church is the Lord's army or Christ's witnesses in this dispensation of grace. It is the body of Christ, from which the bride of Christ will be chosen. It is the empowered church who waited for the coming of the Holy Spirit on the day of Pentecost.

A name mistakenly ascribed to represent the church is the "family of God" (John 1:12). Another term is the "Kingdom of God" (John 3:3). Both terms include those who have been saved and have repented of their sins, but these people cannot represent the church since they haven't obeyed God in the waters of baptism. To belong to the church Christ established, one must not only be saved but also submit to scriptural baptism to show his or her willingness to be identified with the life, works, and sacrifices of the Lord Jesus Christ. This fact is clearly indicated in Acts 2:41. "Then they that gladly received his word were baptized: and the same day there were added unto them about three thousand souls."

For its function, the Bible describes the church as the "body of Christ." This is to signify that every member is a functioning and dynamic constituent interacting with other members to serve his or her leader and master. Each member follows the dictate and will of the head, who is the Lord Jesus Christ. This further indicates that the church isn't an organization that simply gathers members but an organism that has the cognizance to serve and multiply until the Master returns.

The true objective of the church is to propagate its kind. Like a seed, it is expected to grow and multiply not only internally and but also externally, numerically, and exponentially. It must give birth to another church, which then gives birth to another. If a church isn't producing another of the same kind, it isn't fulfilling the purpose God designed for it.

The prayer of this author is that the churches in this generation will not only realize the salvation of individual souls but also establish local churches throughout the world so the souls that will be saved can be nurtured, trained, and equipped as servants of the almighty God to accomplish the greater works He designed for us to do until He comes.

Going, Giving, and Sowing

Music: Hernes M. Abante
Words: Mark Patterson/Hernes Abante
1984

The souls of men are dying.
The heart of God is crying
To tell them of the love of Calvary.

The time is now to reach them
So we'll have time to teach them
About the sacrifice that sets us free.

Chorus:

Lift up your eyes; the fields are white
To harvest now today.
We ask for pow'r that we'll not let
This moment pass away.

Though we may never go there,
The gospel we can sow there
By going, giving, sowing here at home.

Chapter 1
THE JERUSALEM MODEL

In fulfilling the biblical mandate, the International Bible Baptist Church, through the vast and rich experience of this author, has formulated a system of approach in the area of church planting. This system isn't new. None other than the Lord Jesus Himself started it. I call this the "Jerusalem model," which is patterned after the style the Lord and His disciples used, followed through the years, and left for us as an example to emulate and retain. It was used in the first church in Jerusalem; hence the name, the "Jerusalem model."

To fully understand this model, let us trace the development of the Lord's church, the New Testament church, from its conception. It all began based on God's sovereign plan before the foundation of the world when He saw the depravity of humanity, the created beings He cherished from the beginning of creation. Being a compassionate God, He began to express the message of hope—the gospel—beginning in Genesis 3:15. "And I will put enmity between thee and the woman, and between thy seed and her seed; it shall bruise thy head, and thou shalt bruise his heel."

Its fulfillment started when the angelic hosts announced the birth of the Messiah to the shepherds. The angels came with the glorious gospel of the birth of Christ during a time when the world was in total spiritual darkness, without any prophets called on to minister to the people of the world. "And there were in the same country shepherds abiding in the field, keeping watch over their flock by night. And, lo, the angel of the Lord came upon them, and the glory of the Lord shone round about them: and they were sore afraid. And the angel said unto them, Fear not: for, behold, I bring you good tidings of great joy, which shall be to all people" (Luke 2:8–10).

Upon seeing the infant Jesus in the manger, the shepherds "made known abroad the saying which was told them concerning this child." They turned into great evangelists practically overnight. The gospel has never been silent ever since. "And when they had seen it, they made known abroad the saying which was told them concerning this child. And all they that heard it wondered at those things which were told them by the shepherds" (Luke 2:17–18).

As a child, the Lord Jesus lived an ordinary life among people, yet He was and is the Messiah of the world. Like any ordinary young man, He played and talked with ordinary children in the community. He grew up as a normal man, yet he was without sin. He chose to serve people in submission to the will of His heavenly Father. His human experience as a child was to prepare Him for greater challenges in the future as the founder of the New Testament church and the redeemer of all humankind.

His message of hope attracted multitudes of people everywhere He went. When He said, "Follow Me," the disciples followed Him. They abandoned everything and obeyed. People not only heard His voice but also observed how He lived and witnessed the miracles He performed. In spite of His popularity with the crowd, He remained down to earth, humble, and compassionate. He was truly the Word who showed those people in need not only His power and grace but also His mercy.

The Lord didn't stop with the message of salvation. From the start, He taught them obedience by example when He submitted Himself to the baptism of John. Soon after, the apostles and many disciples followed His example and emulated Him in the waters of baptism. After they were baptized, He taught them the whole counsel of God. He taught them how to function and serve.

While the Lord continued to preach and share the message of hope to the lost, He never failed to train and equip the disciples for Christian service. He mentored them with His life, showing them not only how to live but also how to serve with the spirit of compassion and humility. He not only presented a message; He *was* the message and is the message even now.

Jesus started the mentoring approach, which proved to be the most effective way of getting people to follow Him as disciples. They not only learned and lived the truth; they also shared the truth with others.

The results were remarkable. The apostles were followed by more disciples through the continued preaching of the gospel and through personal soul winning. More people were saved and baptized. "The first church grew not only spiritually but also numerically – to the dismay of her (the church's) enemies."

From the first century, the church was recognized neither by the size and beauty of its buildings nor by its physical facilities. Nor did others see it based on its programs and financial resources. Its real asset was people. Despite persecution, the church was on the go with physical and spiritual vigor. It was a mobile church, first within the city of Jerusalem; and then eventually it began to appear in different cities as believers continued to preach and teach.

They met in different places where people could gather. They went everywhere where people were present. They congregated on the seashore with the minister preaching on top of a boat. They were also found meeting in the meadows, under the trees, and in synagogues. Soon they started meeting regularly in houses because of the need to reach and equip others for service. These groups eventually became house churches or congregations scattered all over the city, with the church elders leading them. According to the Bible, the church community had turned, not just Jerusalem but the entire "world upside down" (Acts 17:6), or more appropriately, turned it right side up for the glory of God.

The Test of Faith

With the death of the Lord Jesus Christ, the church suffered a big blow. Seeing soldiers arrest their Master and eventually hang Him on the cross caused the faith of many to shatter. Feeling threatened, they abandoned the Savior to hide for fear of being hunted down and killed like their leader.

However, the Lord Jesus refused to remain in the grave. On the third day, on exactly the day He prophesied, He triumphed and rose from the grave. This glorious event brought the church back to life, this time with greater resolve to perform His will.

When the news reached the ears of the disciples, some believed while others reacted with disbelief—and one named Thomas didn't believe. Nevertheless, hope began to rise again. The disciples became much bolder when they remembered the promise and challenge they had received from the Savior before He died. "Believe you not that I am in the Father, and the Father in me? The words that I speak unto you I speak not of myself: but the Father that dwells in me, he does the works. Believe me that I am in the Father, and the Father in me: or else believe me for the very works' sake. Verily, verily, I say unto you, He that believes on me, the works that I do shall he do also; and greater works than these shall he do; because I go unto my Father" (John 14:10–12).

Soon, the church will reach not only the Jews but also the whole world.

In the beginning, they were told only to reach the Jews, but the message would be different after the resurrection—for they would reach the whole world with the blessed gospel. Their scope would not only be the local area but also stretch as far as the regions beyond.

This was something they had never understood before. On one incident, when they were on their way to Galilee, the Lord decided to go to Samaria. John the Beloved noted this when he wrote what the Lord said while traveling: "And he must needs go through Samaria" (John 4:4).

It was perhaps less than a year since they were instructed to go to only the lost sheep of Israel. "These twelve Jesus sent forth, and commanded them, saying, Go not into the way of the Gentiles, and into any city of the Samaritans enter ye not: But go rather to the lost sheep of the house of Israel" (Matt. 10:5–6).

This development never made sense to them, but their trust in their Master was greater than their confusion. They never realized Jesus would show them another opportunity when He declared that He had "meat to eat that ye know not of" (John 4:31).

The story reveals that they tried to offer Him food, but He refused. It was difficult for them to understand that the "meat" He was telling them about was a new approach, another opportunity—that is, to reach the Samaritans with the gospel. Unbeknownst to them, He had (while the disciples were away, getting food) already started by sowing the seed to the Samaritan woman, who later believed—and who with great excitement began sharing the gospel the same day to the people of Samaria. "The woman then left her waterpot, and went her way into the city, and saith to the men, 'Come, see a man, which told me all things that ever I did: is not this the Christ?'" (John 4:28–29).

It became clear to them when the Lord said in John 4:34, "Jesus saith unto them, My meat is to do the will of him that sent me, and to finish his work."

The disciples already knew of the field of Jerusalem, Judea, and Galilee but not of the field of Samaria. It was a new place, a new world, and a new frontier to conquer for the Lord and for the sake of the lost. What a challenge to go to a place where people were considered outcasts and outsiders. The gospel is also for them. "Say not ye, There are yet four months, and then cometh harvest? behold, I say unto you, Lift up your eyes, and look on the fields; for they are white already to harvest" (John 4:35).

At this time, they began to understand the message of Samaria, especially when the Lord made this very plain in His declaration before His ascension in Matthew 28:19–20. "Go ye therefore, and teach all nations, baptizing them in the name of the Father, and of the Son, and of the Holy Ghost: Teaching them to observe all things whatsoever I have commanded you: and, lo, I am with you alway, even unto the end of the world. Amen."

As the church of the living God, we have the same mandate to fulfill. Let us reach all the people groups with the gospel of the Lord Jesus Christ.

The Empowerment

The Lord wouldn't give a challenging task to the church and expect them to do greater works without help from above. First John 14:10–11 says, "Believest thou not that I am in the Father, and the Father in me? the words that I speak unto you I speak not of myself: but the Father that dwelleth in me, he doeth the works. Believe me that I am in the Father, and the Father in me: or else believe me for the very works' sake."

He declared that we are saved for the "very works' sake." This is the Father's works the Son of God was called to do when He was on this earth. Because they are His works, the church was chosen to complete them.

The works won't be any easier. And to top it off, the Lord declared that He expects us to do "greater works than these" (John 14:12). To accomplish this, He promised in John 14:16–26 the abiding and empowering presence of the Holy Spirit. "And I will pray the Father, and he shall give you another Comforter, that he may abide with you for ever; Even the Spirit of truth; whom the world cannot receive, because it seeth him not, neither knoweth him: but ye know him; for he dwelleth with you, and shall be in you. I will not leave you comfortless: I will come to you.   But the Comforter, which is the Holy Ghost, whom the Father will send in my name, he shall teach you all things, and bring all things to your remembrance, whatsoever I have said unto you."

Although the Holy Spirit is the power, He isn't simply *a* power. He is the third person of the Trinity, and He has a personality. Among all the ministries He does, He has three major works that are significant to the performance of our duties for the Lord:

1. The Holy Spirit's presence indwells all believers.

    This task gives each believer the security and assurance of salvation. The assurance and security of our salvation are designed not only to prepare us for the heavenly place or to make us want to escape from this wicked and corrupt world. They are given to prepare us to serve God more faithfully without any worries about our future.

Ephesians 1:13–14 says, "In whom ye also trusted, after that ye heard the word of truth, the gospel of your salvation: in whom also after that ye believed, ye were sealed with that holy Spirit of promise, Which is the earnest of our inheritance until the redemption of the purchased possession, unto the praise of his glory."

2. The Holy Spirit's presence fills all surrendered believers.

This filling gives believers the power to serve God individually in the local church. It is my sincere opinion, based on the principles of the word of God, that those people who refuse to obey God and refrain from being part of the local church of God have no reason to be filled by the Spirit of God. The filling of the Spirit is intended for personal empowerment so God can use a believer in His service in the local church. Ephesians 5:18 says, "And be not drunk with wine, wherein is excess; but be filled with the Spirit."

3. The Holy Spirit has baptized the corporate body, the church.

The baptism of the Holy Spirit is an act on the corporate body, the church. It occurred only once on the day of Pentecost to empower the church for worldwide effectiveness and testimony. Acts 1:4–8 says,

> And, being assembled together with them, commanded them that they should not depart from Jerusalem, but wait for the promise of the Father, which, saith he, ye have heard of me. For John truly baptized with water; but ye shall be baptized with the Holy Ghost not many days hence. When they therefore were come together, they asked of him, saying, Lord, wilt thou at this time restore again the kingdom to Israel? And he said unto them, It is not for you to know the times or the seasons, which the Father hath put in his own power. But ye

shall receive power, after that the Holy Ghost is come upon you: and ye shall be witnesses unto me both in Jerusalem, and in all Judaea, and in Samaria, and unto the uttermost part of the earth.

God empowered the church when the Holy Spirit filled the very room where the church of 120 faithful and obedient members gathered. It was indeed a baptism of His presence, since His Shekinah glory and power totally saturated the whole place. Acts 2:1–4 says, "And when the day of Pentecost was fully come, they were all with one accord in one place. And suddenly there came a sound from heaven as of a rushing mighty wind, and it filled all the house where they were sitting. And there appeared unto them cloven tongues like as of fire, and it sat upon each of them. And they were all filled with the Holy Ghost, and began to speak with other tongues, as the Spirit gave them utterance."

The baptism of the Holy Spirit or the empowerment of the church resulted in the first great revival, with more than three thousand souls saved and baptized. People from all walks of life and other nations who came to Jerusalem heard the gospel, and the power of God touched and changed them. They went back to their own country, rejoicing. Most of them eventually served as missionaries to the rest of the world.

As mandated, the Jerusalem church continued to flourish. Eventually, James, the half brother of Jesus, became their senior pastor, and under his leadership, preachers were assigned to supervise the flock in different places in the city of Jerusalem. The Bible describes this in Acts 5:42. "And daily in the temple, and in every house, they ceased not to teach and preach Jesus Christ."

Get Out of Your Comfort Zone: Go "Glocal"

After several years, the church began to be comfortable in Jerusalem. The city, which was supposed to be the base of worldwide operations for the gospel and church planting, became their comfort zone. They had forgotten that the gospel is for all and must be propagated to all groups of people all over the world, as Acts 1:8 states.

Since God designed the church to be a worldwide witness, He allowed the church to suffer persecution. This started its dispersion and caused the disciples to scatter, leading to the establishment of many congregations in different localities. Through this, the divine purpose was fulfilled. More churches began to grow and were established. As God's church in this century, let us remember that our mandate is universal and eternal. Let us continue to pursue God's plan.

We usually use the term *local* when we refer to a New Testament church. It's still an appropriate term to use. However, to make the mandate crystal clear, let us use the word *glocal* to describe what a church should be. A "glocal" church is a local church with a global vision. It is what a church must be to fulfill the mandate in Matthew 28:19–20.

The scope of our calling is worldwide. If you are truly called of God, your call extends beyond your locality. The place where God has called you to serve becomes your base of operation, headquarters, and training ground to nurture and equip more servants of the Lord.

Every church must be a "glocal" church. This means each local church has the mandate to reach the whole world, whether your church is in the city or in the province, young or old, rich or poor. Acts 1:8 states that idea clearly with the use of the term *both*, which means "to simultaneously reach Jerusalem, Judea, Samaria, and the uttermost part with the gospel of the Lord."

To make this possible, the Lord sent the Holy Spirit to empower the church not only to carry out the "works" He did but also to complete the "greater works"—a task that is impossible without God's help. The Holy Spirit is here to help us.

Many churches today fail to fulfill the true mandate of the Savior. Most churches are reaching only their kind of people and are confined in one place. Some simply neither believe nor consider the idea of church planting. Others are scared to pioneer a work, perhaps due to lack of experience, resources, and finances. There are those who are willing and passionate but severely lacking in knowledge and understanding.

I trust that this primer will somehow clear up some misconceptions, allay some fears about church planting, and clarify the true design of world mission. It is my prayer and desire to see more churches come out of their sacred walls of isolation and fulfill the mandate to plant churches for the glory of God. This is the essence of the gospel and God's design in winning souls for Christ.

The Great Commission Defined

The Great Commission, as it stands today, is still vague or not identified among the people in our churches. When asked about its description, people talk only about its sequence and scope. For its sequence, we are told only about making disciples and scripturally baptizing and instructing them. For its scope, we are pointed to the whole world. But what does the Great Commission really include? Oh yes, we preach to see people get saved. We want the saved to obey in scriptural baptism, and we want those who are baptized to get full instruction in the whole counsel of God. For what purpose do we want all these goals accomplished in the life of an individual?

Is the Great Commission given only to populate heaven with God's children? Is heaven the ultimate goal of regeneration? Is the goal of the church to give every believer a reason to escape this wicked world, turning the children of God into escapists to go to heaven? No wonder most Christians love to sing the following song:

> This world is not my home, I'm just a-passing through.
> My treasures are laid up somewhere beyond the blue,
> The angels beckon me from heaven's open door,
> And I can't feel at home in this world anymore.[1]

Since we cannot feel at home in this world anymore, we might as well look forward to heaven and escape this wicked and cruel world, right? We forget that God has also instructed us to subdue this earth. Have we forgotten that God gave us this earth and that we should enjoy

---

[1] Excerpt from "This World Is Not My Home," Albert E. Brumley, 1937

this place as long as we are here? Shouldn't we rather sing the song "This Is My Father's World"?

This is my Father's world, and to my listening ears
All nature sings, and 'round me rings the music of the spheres.
This is my Father's world: I rest me in the thought
Of rocks and trees, of skies and seas;
His Hand the wonders wrought.

This is my Father's world, the birds their carols raise,
The morning light, the lily white, declare their Maker's praise.
This is my Father's world: He shines in all that's fair;
In the rustling grass I hear Him pass;
He speaks to me everywhere.

This is my Father's world. O let me ne'er forget
That though the wrong seems oft so strong, God is the ruler yet.
This is my Father's world: why should my heart be sad?
The Lord is King; let the heavens ring!
God reigns; let the earth be glad!

"God is the ruler yet," the song says, so despite the problems and difficulties of life, our hearts must always be glad. As we live, we should focus more on pleasing God and concentrate on the business He has instructed us to perform to finish His works. What a privilege! Praise God!

The Bible clearly states in John 14:11 that we believe God for the "very works sake" and that we should do the "works" that He did. Since the church was instructed to do the "works" of the Lord, it is only proper to identify these "works" that Christ did during His time. What are these works? What do they entail?

Finding the works Christ did during His time in the pages of scripture isn't difficult. The New Testament is a record of all the works He did. The pages of the word of God are full of the supernatural works of the Lord Jesus Christ—works we also need to fulfill through faith and the power of the Holy Spirit. Jesus set Himself up as a model and a miracle worker to follow and emulate, which is why He also mentioned the "greater works" we need accomplish in our lifetimes.

The works the Father assigned Jesus Christ to do were established in Luke 4:18. It states that He was anointed to do these works. These are the messianic works of Christ. As the Lord's representatives and God's messengers in this dispensation of grace, we should also be doing these works:

1. Preaching the gospel to the poor
2. Healing the broken hearted
3. Preaching deliverance to the captives
4. Recovering sight to the blind
5. Setting at liberty those who are bruised

When we consider these works, we get better insight and a clearer understanding of the gospel of the Lord Jesus. Dr. Luke, the disciple who was a doctor and an expert in man's physical needs and condition, gave us the descriptions of the gospel. Through the inspiration of the Holy Spirit, Dr. Luke told us how to reach man effectively. The author of Luke observed this in the person of Jesus during the time he was with the Master. When the Lord was moved with compassion in Matthew 9:36, this was because He saw the condition of their souls. He referred not only to one's eternal destiny but also to the needs and quality of the second element in man, the soul.

First Thessalonians 5:23 reveals man's trichotomous nature. Man is made up of spirit, soul, and body. "And the very God of peace sanctify you wholly; and I pray God your whole spirit and soul and body be preserved blameless unto the coming of our Lord Jesus Christ."

1. Spirit is the spiritual aspect of man, the God consciousness. It is given for man to have the opportunity to communicate with God. It returns to God. Ecclesiastes 12:7 says, "Then shall the dust return to the earth as it was: and the spirit shall return unto God who gave it."

People in their natural state are spiritually dead. The biblical definition of *death* is "separation." It doesn't mean they are void of spirit. Rather, their spirits are separated from their soul so they cannot communicate spiritual things.

When people are regenerated or saved, the Holy Spirit quickens their spirits. They become alive, and so they begin to communicate to the souls. The quickened spirit of people is the residence of the Holy Spirit that communicates to the soul of people the things of God. It can now influence the soul.

2. The soul is the real person, the self-consciousness.

   It is the seat of man's mind, emotion, and will. It is the eternal and responsible part of people. The soul who isn't saved is void of righteousness because the spirit is separated. He or she always thinks, loves, and decides contrary to God. However, souls who are saved have the capability of thinking godly, loving godly, and deciding godly because their spirits communicate to their souls. They are alive. Their destiny is heaven. The destiny of the unsaved soul is hell.

3. The body is the physical aspect of man.

   It is the reflection of man's inner self. It is also called the shell or the mortal part of man that goes back to dust upon death. The body translates what the mind thinks, the heart emotes, and the will decides into action. However, the body that is shed in death will also rise up in the resurrection day.

   The purpose of the gospel is that the Holy Spirit, through the word of God, will quicken the human spirit, which will then quicken the soul (the seat of the mind, emotion, and volition) and cause the body to act (to translate into actions). It is never about the eternal destiny or place called heaven. The purpose of the gospel is to turn mortal people into spiritual beings like Christ. The goal is Christlikeness.

We do the works of the Lord to reach the souls of man. Take note that the five works in Luke 4:18 talk about the need and condition of the mind, emotion, and will of man. The first refers to those who are poor in spirit, the first ones who need spiritual rehabilitation. For the purpose of clarification, let me explain each one:

A. Preaching the gospel to the poor: The word of God talks about the poor in spirit, people whose spirits are not quickened and are unresponsive to the truth. This is the first that needs to be addressed among the needs of man. This is the soul-winning part most Christians are involved in. However, sadly, this is the only need most churches are addressing. Most people stop here, but there is more. The quickened spirits should become God's bold warriors and mighty servants to accomplish the works of the Lord.

B. Healing the broken hearted: The salvation experience doesn't automatically erase all the heartaches and emotional needs of the individual. However, it can provide the power to overcome and be victorious in fighting the emotional battle plaguing all believers. Most Christians are unable to fulfill the will of God and finish the works of the Lord because of emotional and psychological problems. We need to help fight this battle so they can serve the Lord better.

C. Preaching deliverance to the captives: When the Lord mentioned captives, He had the obsessed in mind, people who are addicted to vices, which cause significant problems in this world. Having this kind of captivity makes people unable to totally surrender to the will of God because they are under the influence of another power, not necessarily of Satan but of self. It is our duty to help release them from this form of captivity. When they are free, then they can serve the Lord with greater freedom.

D. Recovering sight to the blind: This doesn't necessarily refer to unbelievers. Notice the word *recover*. It means the blind person was seeing at one point in time and then was blinded, perhaps by the things of the world. There are many Christians in this predicament. They no longer see through God's eyes because they have allowed the affairs of men to blind them. It is our duty to make them see again so they can serve God more faithfully.

E. Setting at liberty them that are bruised: We have many people who are hurting because of the violence present in this world: physical, emotional, and psychological. Hence, people are helpless and scared, unable to move. We need to reach them with the hope in Christ. They need healing and closure so they can serve God with greater freedom.

Understanding the works God has given the local church will help every pastor reach and train the people of God. It will help every member of the church to be more responsible in the works of the Lord, knowing that the tasks are clear and focused. There should be no second-guessing the ministry or approaching it by means of trial and error. This is the "holistic" approach: targeting the total person and making every person fully equipped to serve God.

Second Timothy 3:14–17 says, "But continue thou in the things which thou hast learned and hast been assured of, knowing of whom thou hast learned them; And that from a child thou hast known the holy scriptures, which are able to make thee wise unto salvation through faith which is in Christ Jesus. All scripture is given by inspiration of God, and is profitable for doctrine, for reproof, for correction, for instruction in righteousness: That the man of God may be perfect, throughly furnished unto all good works."

Chapter 2
FEARS AND CONCERNS IN CHURCH PLANTING

Every church leader has a desire to be successful. In terms of success, a pastor wants to see not only a good crowd but also a nice church building with all the features of comfort and other amenities to keep members comfortable where they are. Unfortunately, the comfort and convenience of the people have become the major concern. Most churches try to please people more than they please the Lord. Hence, they tend to give to the people whatever they demand, because of the belief that having these comfortable features and the number of people they attract (despite their unwillingness to serve) speaks of success.

Consequently, when the church has all the facilities, the crowd, and the comfort, a pastor isn't likely to let go of anybody. Everyone and everything have to stay. The focus is no longer on the mandate to reach the lost but on the desire to protect and keep what has been attained and obtained. Many churches no longer do the job of building up people. They merely maintain what they have. The result is a lack of excitement and spiritual direction among members, which causes them to maintain the status quo without the motivation to go and plant churches.

However, that isn't the main concern. The main problem is when pastors themselves aren't motivated to expand the work. This is when they become more concerned about establishing and enlarging their own kingdom than expanding and propagating the kingdom of God.

Hindrances to Church Planting

The following are some reasons why pastors and churches aren't interested in planting more churches and congregations:

1. The church doesn't want to lose the mature and faithful members who are qualified to go and start a work. They feel that this will adversely affect the church when they leave.
2. The church doesn't want to lose tithing members since they are the generous givers.
3. The church doesn't want to lose quality leaders and faithful servants. To let go of these people would mean to lose the backbone of the church.
4. The church doesn't want to lose money, since starting mission works and outreach congregations can and will deplete the church finances.
5. The church has lost its pioneering spirit. Nowadays, many preachers are no longer interested in pioneering a church due to fear of the difficulty in starting a work. The pioneering spirit has been lost, a quality needed to be successful in church planting. Pastoral candidates and fresh Bible college graduates are merely interested in looking for ready positions, income, and ministerial benefits. They are applying for a position instead of establishing a church. The ministry is no longer a spiritual vocation; it's simply a profession to earn a living.

The current style of many church-planting efforts is to use humanistic and secular business techniques. The approach is as though a worldly business enterprise for profit were being started. The International Bible Baptist Church and Ministry follows a biblical pattern, a God-honoring approach. It is an approach based on faith and obedience. In the ministry, I have learned that faith must not be based on a burden one feels to start a ministry; then when there is no burden, there is no action. It must be simple obedience to what God has commanded. If the Lord expects a church to start other churches, then we must believe that members and leaders should be trained and equipped with that goal in mind.

Throughout the history of the church, God has been using laypeople to start churches. These eventually became pastors and leaders of the congregations. Some decide to train men who are saved in their ministry. With effective training and mentoring, these are then given the pastoral responsibilities. This approach avoids the hiring of pastors from the outside who never have true compassion and the drive to lead the people unless they get a good-paying job with full benefits. I haven't done a scientific study of the numbers of hired pastors in churches in any given place in today's generation. I believe, however, that it is safe to say that more than 70 percent of churches in the USA (maybe more) are now led by people hired from the outside or fresh from a Bible school. We have developed modern "Balaams" in our generation. It is sad to say that we are allowing this trend to go unchallenged.

Some pastors, even the pioneers, merely focus on establishing a spiritual empire. Their aim is to leave behind a personal legacy of success. This is a self-serving approach. It aims only to satisfy, empower, enrich, maintain, protect, and provide comfort and financial stability to the leader or founder of the church without considering the needs of the people. These churches are totally beholden to one powerful leader who lacks a servant's heart. These are leaders whose shoes no one else can fill. They have made it difficult for another to take their place. They have merely trained followers to show loyalty ascribed only to them. They don't plant churches. Rather, they start "occupations" or spiritual "territories." These churches eventually die with the demise of their powerful leaders.

Today, the only involvement most churches have in regard to church planting and world missions is by financially supporting the program of another church engaged in sending out church planters and missionaries. They don't find the need to send someone from their local congregations to physically go to the mission field. They think that sending money and resources constitutes the idea of going. They are comfortably and conveniently piggyback riding on the mission project of another congregation. Yet they feel they are obeying the command to go.

As much as possible, churches keep their members within their backyard. They are afraid to release or send them out, since this means losing quality members along with their financial commitment. New workers and preachers aren't being groomed and trained due to shortsightedness and lack of encouragement. Instead of building churches for the spiritual edification of individual members, they build physical buildings and beautiful facilities to show an appearance of success and accomplishment and to make the members feel comfortable. The church becomes another comfort zone.

Other churches start Bible colleges and schools, which inadvertently siphon faithful workers and potentially capable leaders from the churches where they belong for many years, requiring students to serve in their ministry. The pastors of churches with nearby schools use students from small churches as church workers. These Bible college students surrendered their lives with the original intention of going back to their home churches. Sadly, what usually happens is that they remain in the school to serve, forgetting what they committed to the church where they came from. They forgot the church that encouraged and prayed for them. These churches use the efforts of others to fulfill their desires in the name of the ministry.

On the other hand, some pastors strongly believe in the principle of church planting but are afraid to lose excellent workers and income. The thought of losing their treasured preachers and members for another work freezes them. They feel that keeping them within the neighborhood is more important than sending them out to start a brand-new work. They are also afraid to venture out since it will incur additional expenses such as the rental of a facility, pastoral support, and so forth.

A church that doesn't grow outwardly will become destitute inwardly. It will die from the inside. Any God-called man can start a church and see an increase in attendance in just a few years. But what is the guarantee that the church will remain to grow and even continue to exist until the return of Christ? Many things can possibly happen. The church will grow, remain the same, split up, or be totally dissolved. If it remains, it will have an impact only in the place where it is located. It will reach only its Jerusalem or maybe its Judea.

The work of church planting, if done properly, will provide greater opportunities to grow, expand, and reach a greater number of people, since congregations will be spread out in different communities. The result is more positive. There is continuous progress in growth and expansion. Although we don't adhere to the marketing strategy of many so-called fast-food restaurants, we do find more success in small franchises compared to a large fine-dining restaurant with only one branch. These small franchises serve a greater number of people. I can see that they have learned this principle from the New Testament.

The establishment of local churches or congregations is more important than building business franchises. What a church planter must have in fulfilling this mandate is total faith in God. He needs to totally depend on God's power and plan. Faith simply means believing and obeying what God has declared for us to do. I am an embodiment of what God can do in the life of an undeserving servant of God.

My Personal Testimony of Faith and Service

I came to the United States as a student with a personal and selfish ambition. There is nothing wrong with anybody wanting to come to the United States to pursue a particular field of study. However, when you use a student visa to escape from a responsibility, like Jonah of old, that is a major problem.

I began serving in the church at an early age. Being a pastor's kid gave me exposure to the works of the ministry, especially in the area of music, Good News Clubs, and Sunday school. It is a fact that I started being involved in church work even before my salvation. I made a profession of faith when I was eight years old through the encouragement of my mother, but I did so without a full understanding of what it truly means to be saved. During a camp in Baguio, while playing the accordion during an invitation, I realized I wasn't really born again. I vividly remember the message Dr. Bob Hughes gave that night. It was a message about time. I remember him using a measuring tape to illustrate the time we spend for self against the time we spend for God. That message made me realize God wasn't using my whole life. Yes, I was involved in church, but since my heart wasn't in it and I wasn't really saved, everything was done only for self.

Since I was playing the invitation song, I was too embarrassed to approach the altar until the Spirit gave me the boldness to go, not realizing that Dr. Bob Hughes was already waiting for me; he had already noticed that I was in tears and deeply convicted. When I finally approached the altar, he gave me a tight hug, prayed with me, and encouraged me to do the right thing. That very night, I not only received the assurance of salvation but also surrendered to the Lord's ministry.

That experience changed my perception about life and the church. The more involved I became in the work of the Lord, I started seeing the Lord open doors of opportunities for service. I became a church pianist, youth leader, music director, home Bible study leader, and preacher. I was one of the first graduates of Asia Baptist Bible College in Sta. Mesa, Manila. The Lord allowed me to finish Bible college in 1974 at the top of my class.

In 1976, I was the assistant to my father, the late Dr. Ben O. Abante Sr., who started the Banawe Bible Baptist Mission, which later became Lighthouse Bible Baptist Church. As the assistant pastor, I was the first youth and music director. I was also actively involved in campus work, having started Bible study groups with the help of our students at the University of the Philippines, Philippine Women's University, Ateneo University, Central Colleges of the Philippines, Eulogio Amang Rodriguez University, and other high school campuses. Some students whom the gospel of the Lord Jesus reached are now serving the Lord in a pastoral capacity. God's grace has allowed me to work with several young people who are now faithfully serving Him. That was one part of my spiritual life and journey.

In spite of all the blessings I received in the ministry, my mind wouldn't let go of the unfairness and unfavorable treatment toward our family in the past, especially against my father. During the heat of the attacks coming from people we thought loved us, the time came when I made a personal commitment to take my family out of misery by going to the States and pursuing a career so I could help the family and ministry not depend on these people anymore. This led me to aggressively pursue another career outside God's will.

Unbeknownst to most people, including my parents, I was living another life—one focused on my personal ambition to be famous and rich. I was pursuing a career in show business. While teaching music at Grace Christian School and working as assistant pastor of Lighthouse Bible Baptist Church, I was also performing and working professionally in the field of secular music. I was then finishing a bachelor of music degree in the College of Music and Fine Arts (CMFA) with three scholarships. They were from the Don Timotheo Certeza Educational Foundation (academic), the Felicing Tirona Music Foundation (voice), and the CMFA Scholarship (music). My college education was free, and at the same time, I was enjoying some form of popularity. I had a taste of the world, and I ate it as well. I performed publicly incognito, afraid that my father, the person I respected so much, would discover me. I was afraid that my worldly involvement would destroy my testimony and eventually the ministry my father had worked so hard for.

Feeling that I was caught in a whirlpool of the world, I planned to escape. For fear of being exposed and eventually destroying my father's ministry due to my growing involvement with the world (and at the same time becoming unhappy with the work of the Lord), I started, in a quiet and subtle way, to save money and apply to go to the USA as a student. To make my move spiritually credible, I applied not only at the universities but also at several seminaries offering a master's degree in theology, education, and music. I was accepted. On September 20, 1980, I boarded the PAL flight to San Francisco to make it to the fall semester. Only a week prior to my departure, I mentioned my secret agenda to my father for the first time. He had no choice but to let me go.

Life in the USA

Coming to the USA was a risky and adventurous move. I had only $1,000 in my pocket (money I had secretly saved), a scholarship offer from a school, and a commitment from friends in San Francisco to help me out with board and lodging. It was a bold move since I didn't know that God, through His grace, was in control of the situation. He was already paving a different way for me.

Faced with the reality of being in a foreign country and not knowing anybody in another state where another school had accepted me as a student, I was forced to stay in the Bay Area in California. I accepted the offer of a full scholarship from an old local seminary in the city of San Francisco. I was also offered a position as the music director of a local Baptist church with an apartment provision and a regular monthly income of $300; it was an offer too good to refuse. The choice also enabled me to stay in San Francisco, close to my childhood friends. I found myself back in the church and in the music ministry. In the seminary, I found myself confronting issues about God and Christian service. I was again under the ministry of the word of God. Truly, the Lord's calling has no repentance.

Soon, by God's grace, my spiritual vigor was rekindled. I recommitted my life to God. After finishing my seminary studies, I was hired as a music director at the Bible Baptist Church in Marysville, California. I was glad to accept the position when I learned that the church was a member of the Baptist Bible Fellowship International, a fellowship where I originally belonged, a missionary organization the Lord had used to reach my family with the gospel.

I remained in that church, serving as an assistant pastor for six years. Later, upon the resignation of the senior pastor, I was unofficially asked to serve as the pastor in charge for almost one year until another pastor was hired to take over the work. Less than two years later, the Lord called me to pioneer a work in Suisun City, California. With my wife and daughter, Naomi, in tow, we left Marysville by faith and started the International Bible Baptist Mission in our garage in September 1997.

The Birth of the International Bible Baptist Mission

Like a mother going through severe labor pangs before the birth of a child, I, too, have undergone a lot of difficulties. When I was working as the music director and then the assistant pastor at a Bible Baptist church, I felt so welcomed, loved, and cherished. I was respected, praised, and allowed to preach, teach, sing, play the piano, and share a testimony in several churches and mission conferences. However, when I announced my desire to establish a New Testament church, everything changed. I was told to go back to the Philippines. I was discouraged, even by the very people who had praised and prayed for me. I was told that the USA wasn't my place to start a work, that I wouldn't be effective in ministering to the Americans, and that it wasn't right for me to focus only on Asians with the gospel. I felt rejected and totally misunderstood. I was devastated and became disillusioned. I became resentful of the Baptist Bible Fellowship.

I remember trying to raise my support with three other church planters in Northern California. One went to Berkeley, California, and one went to another known city. These three were able to raise enough support, ranging from $1,500 to $3,000 a month. I was able to raise only $160 a month, and the majority of the amount came from my sending church. I honestly didn't know how to take all the criticisms. Was it racial, or was it a stance to discourage me in staying in America? Although I initially reacted negatively, I eventually decided to accept the criticism as God's will and to trust the Lord completely.

The overwhelming financial need didn't encourage me to quit the ministry or go back to my old country, the Philippines. The fighter I am decided, by God's grace, to prove all of them wrong. At that time, my father was also persuading me to return to the Philippines to assist him in the work of the Lord. That would have been a convenient move for me. However, I knew then that God wanted me to start a work in the States. I was totally confident of my divine calling to start a church.

To make ends meet financially for my family, I worked in the post office on the graveyard shift as a letter machine operator. This I did for the first six years as the pastor of International Bible Baptist Church

(IBBC). Then for the next decade, I served as a child abuse investigator and senior social worker at Solano Child Protective Services. I considered these jobs as a blessing from the Lord. Despite the hectic schedule, they didn't take my time away from concentrating on the ministry.

Five years ago, I quit my social worker job to concentrate on the growing ministry. I praise God for the jobs He gave. They supported me through the difficult times. They provided the benefits I needed for my family and me, such as medical and dental benefits, insurance, and a retirement fund. During the time I was working the other jobs, the church supported me financially. IBBC started doing that not because I needed the support but because they believed it was their responsibility to financially support the man of God. These funds allowed me to give more financially to the work of the Lord. Now the church is currently providing all my needs and benefits.

The ministry isn't without difficulties. I encountered a lot of them from the beginning. This experience proves only that the work of the Lord cannot depend on the ability and wisdom of man. God's works are supernatural and can be accomplished only through His faith and power. I learned this truth early in the ministry. I learned to trust God in all things, even in simple things. I learned that the ministry isn't about what I can do or what I can afford to give and do. It's all about what the Lord can do.

The first difficulty I had in pioneering a work was how to reach people for Christ. I knew nobody when I moved my family to Solano County to start a work. I passed this place while on our way to a family camp years ago. The place immediately left an impression on my heart. From then on, I knew God wanted us to go there to start a work.

It was a move of faith. The first thing I did was saturating my neighborhood. I knocked on doors and introduced the new ministry to families I met. While knocking on some doors in my neighborhood, I stumbled across a family looking for a church. The husband was Paul Kellogg. The person who had led him to the Lord had advised him to look for a local Baptist church. When I introduced myself as a pastor looking to start a church in the area, Paul opened his home for a Bible study. That led to the salvation of his wife, two children, and his mother-in-law. The following Sunday, I baptized them at Fellowship Baptist Church in Vacaville, California. With this family, the International Bible Baptist Mission (IBBM) was born in October 2007.

The young congregation met regularly in our home in Suisun City. Eventually, we moved to our garage, where we arranged the place into a small auditorium, meeting every Sunday morning at ten o'clock. Soon many souls were added and baptized into the mission, including a couple, Danny and Agnes Decena. Danny was already a believer and brought his wife, Agnes, to the Bible study; and on the same day, she got saved.

This couple was instrumental in the salvation of another family from Alameda, California, the Toribio family. Through the efforts of Danny and Agnes, I was invited one Saturday evening to a home Bible study in the home of Gil Toribio and his family. I remember their home having several images of saints and other Catholic paraphernalia on the walls. By the grace of God, about a dozen souls were saved that night. The following week, they all followed the Lord in the waters of baptism. Their home became another home Bible study ministry. Brother Gil Toribio became my first preacher in the ministry, and his wife, Felicia, became a faithful soul winner and Sunday school worker.

The Organization of IBBC

On February 7, 1998, just less than four months from the start of IBBM, the International Bible Baptist Church was organized into an independent ministry. A total of fifty-seven members signed the original charter with Dr. Brad Weniger, the pastor of the Bible Baptist Church, our sending church, officiating. That day I was installed as the pastor of the new church. Over one hundred people attended that historical event at the senior center in Suisun City.

The next several years were challenging. To survive, IBBC moved to ten different locations to hold worship services. From my garage, we moved to the Suisun City Senior Center, the Fairfield Library, the Vallejo Filipino Community Center, Alameda College, another garage in Alameda, the Toribio family home, the All Nations Fellowship Church facility, the Calvary Baptist Church facility in Alameda, a Methodist church facility, and finally a storefront at East 14th Street in San Leandro, California. Then we purchased the present property the church is occupying today. Every time the church moved, members were displaced, consequently leading to discouragement and eventually losing them to another church.

The Beginning of Outreach Congregations

To keep the people from leaving, I started the outreach ministry. IBBC began to start local congregations in four key locations around the main church to encourage the members to stay in their locality, thus remaining with IBBC. While they are still encouraged to attend the main worship service on Sunday morning, separate worship services were being held in their locality. In the evening, five separate worship services occurred simultaneously around the Bay Area. I remember traveling and preaching in three different places every Sunday. This situation eventually prompted me to start training preachers through the Bible institute program. As we saw the effectiveness of this approach, the church planting ministry was born.

All the men of IBBC are encouraged to be spiritual leaders and Bible study leaders, so when a family moves to another location and cannot find a church of like faith and practice, they can start a home Bible study that will eventually become another IBBC congregation. When we see a family move to another place, we don't lose that family; we gain a congregation. Soon IBBC was starting not only outreaches but also mission congregations and churches in various cities and states. This trend expanded to other countries: the Philippines and Canada.

Right now the International Bible Baptist Ministry has twenty-seven congregations in mainland USA, Hawaii, Canada, and the Philippines. The goal of the ministry is to start three new congregations every year, and so far the Lord has been helping to fulfill this goal. In 2008, three congregations were started in Los Angeles, California: IBBC Riverside, IBBC Sta. Clarita, and IBBC Fresno. The year before, in 2007, IBBC started IBBC Vancouver, Canada, and two congregations in the Philippines: IBBC Kabankalan and IBBC Tacurong.

To maintain the momentum, the IBBC ministry sponsors an annual church planting conference in San Leandro, California, to maintain the awareness about the need of planting new congregations. In 2008, the conference was also held in the Philippines, and a partnership was started with other ministries, such as Blue Ridge Bible Baptist Church, Lighthouse Bible Baptist Church, and Metropolitan Bible Baptist Church. I expect this partnership to produce many more congregations all over the world by God's grace.

This year, IBBC hopes to pioneer a church in the southern border, the country of Mexico, through the help of our missionary there, Brother Ramon Lukban. Other places of opportunity this year are the states of Alaska, Washington, Connecticut, and New York. We also hope to begin another ministry in Canada and in more cities in the Philippines. To God be the glory!

Chapter 3
REQUIREMENTS FOR CHURCH PLANTERS

In any vocation or profession, there are requirements and tools needed. Church planters are no different. They need to be equipped with certain qualifications and knowledge to use the tools of trade and resources to do the job right. No people, no matter how spiritual they are, can presume that they can start a church without these important requirements to make the work better secured and established. I say this because I have heard some spiritually minded people claim that the only thing they need is the power of the Spirit of God. That sounds very spiritual, but the Holy Spirit, omnipotent and omniscient as He is, won't go against the will of the Father. He won't work against the requirements of the word of God. Many successful, experienced, and Spirit-filled church planters who had been there before us gave us a great example to follow and made it easier for the next generation. Let us learn from them.

The following are the basic requirements and tools you need as a church planter:

Biblical Requirements

Church planters must be assured not only of their salvation but also of their calling in the Lord's ministry. A special calling isn't necessary to start a church since the Bible has already given the command for what has to be done as well as why and how. However, the leading of the Spirit, I believe, is necessary in the area of location and logistics.

There is also a general call given to all God's people, and everyone must obey that call, one of which is soul winning. We are all commanded to win souls. This is not only the responsibility of the preachers and church leaders but also the duty of every individual under the authority of the local church. It is threefold: salvation of the lost, baptism, and discipleship. This threefold approach is the preparation every believer needs to meet to be equipped in doing the works of the Lord, established in Luke 4:18. In fulfilling this, new converts must be ushered into a local church to allow spiritual growth and to be given the opportunity to serve God. Soul winners can never do their work apart from the local church.

Church planters must not only focus on the works to experience victory in reaching the needs of individuals and to train them to serve God effectively. They must also have the genuine attitude and desire in their hearts to accomplish the works of the Lord. Here are some biblical requirements church planters must meet:

Spiritual Passion or the Love of God to Serve

Romans 10:1 says, "Brethren, my heart's desire and prayer to God for Israel is, that they might be saved." Spiritual passion is an intense feeling from the heart of doing something that is not only good but also right for the sake of others. It comes with compelling action inspired by the love of God. It is different from an ordinary desire coming from the natural heart without the influence of God. To have spiritual passion is to have the unconditional love of God. It isn't to love just for the sake of loving but to love for a godly and noble reason.

To have spiritual passion is not only about having a feeling or emotion. There is a compelling need to act on that desire. The action is doing whatever is necessary to satisfy the object of that desire. In this case, the object of passion is God, and the recipients of that desire are the people He loves us to reach. Church planters must have this spiritual quality. Without this, a man of God cannot endure the cross of discouragement and the heights of victory that come with the service of the Lord.

Knowledge of the Word of God

Second Timothy 3:15 says, "And that from a child thou hast known the Scriptures, which are able to make thee wise unto salvation through faith which is in Christ Jesus." The knowledge and understanding of the scriptures is paramount in the service of the Lord. Since the Bible is the basis of our faith and practice, we cannot do the work of the Lord without its power and influence. Church planters must be in love with God's word. Its influence must fully saturate their total being: spirit, soul, and body. They must be in God's word daily.

A Teachable Attitude

Proverbs 9:9 says, "Give instruction to a wise man, and he will be yet wiser: teach a just man, and he will increase in learning." A person with childlike faith has a very teachable heart. It is the quality of a person having a teachable spirit and fully surrendering to the will and instructions of the Lord. A person who has a teachable attitude can be under the instructions of anybody God wants to use to teach him or her. Having a teachable attitude makes one willing to learn, even from a child and from any experiences or circumstances God will allow along the way. It is having a mind open to God's instructions and directions.

Humility

First Peter 5:6 says, "Humble yourselves therefore under the mighty hand of God, that He might exalt you in due time." Humility is the quality of having one's will fully surrendered to the will of God. A strong self-will is what makes a person proud, but a surrendered will is what makes him or her humble. The man of God must have the latter. The Bible tells us to have the mind of God. Jesus Christ is the best example of humility because although He is God, He still submitted to the will of the heavenly Father.

Empathy

Second Corinthians 5:21 says, "For He hath made Him to be sin for us, who knew no sin; that we might be made the righteousness of God in Him." An empathetic relationship is needed to fully understand the need of man. This isn't simply an act of sharing feelings with another but feeling what others feel to bring comfort and assurance. It means carrying the burden of another and putting himself or herself in another man's shoes. This is a vicarious relationship, just like what Christ did on the cross. "He became sin for us." A man of God who has empathy is willing to take the place of another to feel and experience his or her sufferings and difficulties.

Servitude

Matthew 23:11 says, "But he that is greatest among you shall be your servant." Servant leadership is what spiritual leadership is all about. In the work of the Lord, one isn't qualified to be a leader unless he or she is first willing to be a servant. This is the quality of having the attitude of submission and obedience to another leader as he or she leads others. It is the acceptance of this fact: one can never reach a point where he or she reaches the top of the world. Whatever distance or heights people attain, they are always under another leader, and the leader is always God.

Sacrifice

Romans 12: 1 says that "ye present your bodies a living sacrifice, holy, acceptable unto God, which is your reasonable service." Sacrifice is the quality in people to let go of what is dear, important, and significant in life. It is a willingness to get hurt for the sake of others. The secular world is centered on getting instead of giving. Giving can also be selfish if the desire is to get something in return.

Sacrifice is different. We give more of what we can afford so we give more of ourselves. What we give simply cannot be replaced because we give part of ourselves. The work of the Lord is a life of sacrifice. A church planter must be willing to sacrifice to succeed.

Faith in God

Hebrews 11:6 says, "But without faith it is impossible to please Him." To exercise faith is to know and understand God's purpose and desire. God gives faith because His desire is to work in and through us. If He intends for us to work within our human abilities and understanding, then we don't need faith. This isn't to say He doesn't want to use the faculties He has given us, because He has given those to us for His own use. Our job is to surrender everything to Him.

Hebrews 11:6 says, "Without faith it is impossible to please God." This means that to live by faith, we need to let go of our control and allow God to take full control so He can accomplish greater and mighty things for His glory, beyond our abilities and understanding. Even in the area of giving, it is God who gives through us ... more than what we can afford.

The work of the Lord is a supernatural task. Our natural abilities and wisdom cannot accomplish it. Faith allows us to move, act, work, give, and accomplish things beyond our abilities and control.

Initiative and Creativity

First Thessalonians 4:11 says, "And that ye study to be quiet, and to do your own business, and to work with your own hands." Those who have initiative are willing to work independently and interdependently without waiting to be instructed or told. They have the capability of thinking and using their understanding and skills to initiate a move with confidence, knowing what they are doing is totally within the tasks.

Creativity is the work of an artisan. A man of God is an artist who creates something that is totally glorifying to God.

Ability to Work and Train Leaders

Second Timothy 2:2 says, "And the things that thou has heard among many witnesses, the same commit thou to faithful men, who shall be able to teach others also." A man of God must not be insecure of his calling and profession. He must be willing to train somebody who can replace him someday. He should be a leader of leaders, willing to transfer the knowledge and skills he has attained to another. To be an effective church planter, learn to develop more church planters.

Strong Biblical Conviction

Ephesians 4:14 says, "That we henceforth be no more children, tossed to and fro, and carried about with every wind of doctrine." With the popularity of generic Christianity, we seldom find people in our generation willing to stand on the truth of God's word. Even pastors have turned mute and quiet when it comes to certain truths such as the inspiration and preservation of the scripture, the local church, the deity of Christ, the virgin birth of the Lord, biblical morality, and the bride of Christ. Consequently, Christians have turned weak in their doctrinal stand and unstable in their moral convictions. As God's servants, we need to show strength, firmly grounded on the solid foundation of God's word. People depend on what we preach and on the lives we live.

Ability and Willingness to Multitask

First Timothy 3:1–5 says, "This is a true saying, if a man desire the office of a bishop, he desireth a good work. A bishop then must be blameless, the husband of one wife … One that ruleth well his own house, having his children in subjection … For if a man know how to rule his own house, how shall he take care of the church of God."

The man of God handles several positions of responsibilities. He is a husband, father, counselor, teacher, preacher, administrator, community leader, social worker, employee, employer, and so forth. Without the ability and willingness to multitask, the work of the Lord can be overwhelming to handle and can result in total burnout. A church planter must know how to juggle or move from one position and responsibility to another without compromising individual responsibilities.

Physical and Emotional Requirements

The Bible declares that one's body is the "temple of the Holy Spirit" (1 Corinthians 6:19) and therefore must be presented as a "living sacrifice," (Romans 12:1) not a weak or dying sacrifice. Many preachers don't take good care of their bodies and mental health. They feel their only responsibility is to have healthy spiritual lives. A weak mind and body cannot maintain and sustain a healthy spiritual life. In the same token, a sound spirit produces a healthy mind and body. First Thessalonians 5:23 says, "And the very God of peace sanctify you wholly; and I pray God your whole spirit and soul and body be preserved blameless unto the coming of our Lord Jesus Christ."

The above passage declares that we are not only spiritual beings but also physical beings with souls where emotions, wills, and intelligence reside. That fact makes us trichotomous beings composed of spirits, souls, and bodies. We therefore have a responsibility to maintain not only our spirits but also our physical and mental well-being.

An active spiritual life can influence the mind, which can then move the body into action. A healthy spirit nourishes the soul and body. Others can see a healthy spirit through the body's action and the attitude of the soul (emotions, wills, intelligence). A dynamic and nourished spirit will have a positive effect on the mind, will, and emotions. We can maintain a total state of health in the following three areas:

1. Spiritually: We must allow the principles of godliness to influence our lives. These spiritual and biblical principles must communicate to our total being, thus making the word of God relevant and true in our daily existence.

2. Bodily: Though we are spiritual beings, we are still mortals, subject to human weaknesses and human limitations. Let us take care of our physical homes so we can function properly and live to serve God.

3. Mentally: We should learn not to worry and to be always in moderation when facing the different issues of life. For good mental health, we must claim the following verses in Philippians 4:4–9:

Rejoice in the Lord alway: and again I say, Rejoice. Let your moderation be known unto all men. The Lord is at hand. Be careful for nothing; but in everything by prayer and supplication with thanksgiving let your requests be made known unto God. And the peace of God, which passeth all understanding, shall keep your hearts and minds through Christ Jesus. Finally, brethren, whatsoever things are true, whatsoever things are honest, whatsoever things are just, whatsoever things are pure, whatsoever things are lovely, whatsoever things are of good report; if there be any virtue, and if there be any praise, think on these things. Those things, which ye have both learned, and received, and heard, and seen in me, do: and the God of peace shall be with you.

Knowledge of the Truth

I slightly touched on this issue at the beginning of this primer. Let me explore it more extensively in this chapter, because I consider it to be very significant in church planting. When we talk about the truth, we refer to the word of God: the source of all truths and the basis of our faith and practice. A friend of mine has made an acronym of the word BIBLE: Basic Instructions before Leaving Earth

We need to be familiar with the book of instructions God has left us so we can live our lives according to His will and desires. The purpose of learning the truth isn't for self-gratification. We learn so we can teach others also. This truth is clearly stated in 2 Timothy 2:2. "And the things that thou hast heard of me among many witnesses, the same commit thou to faithful men, who shall be able to teach others also."

Passion for the lost is a great motivation to be in the ministry, but that alone won't prepare one for the tasks. A church planter also needs knowledge to effectively pursue his or her calling. It is equally true that you will never be successful in the ministry with knowledge alone. You also need passion to balance the equation.

Passion without knowledge will bring frustration and can cause severe burnout. Knowledge, on the other hand, without passion will bring pride and arrogance. Since it is assumed that all those in the ministry are there because of passion for the lost, let us then explore the need of knowledge in this chapter.

The apostle Paul, in preparing his young disciple Timothy for the ministry, wrote two epistles to tell him it was important to prepare and be equipped for the job. In 1 Timothy, the apostle Paul focused on the questions of church order, soundness of faith, and discipline. The key phrase in this epistle is found in 1 Timothy 3:15. "But if I tarry long, that thou mayest know how thou oughtest to behave thyself in the house of God, which is the church of the living God, the pillar and ground of the truth."

The second epistle encourages Timothy to study. Second Timothy 2:15 says, "Study to shew thyself approved unto God, a workman that needeth not to be ashamed, rightly dividing the word of truth.

How then do we study? Is self-study enough to learn? Should one study under a mentor? Does one need to enroll in an institute or a Bible college? These are some questions a lot of preachers are faced with.

One of the names given to a follower of the Lord Jesus Christ is "disciple." It means a "learner, scholar, or one who receives instruction from another." A disciple works closely with a discipler or mentor. Since every believer in Christ must seek to know the truth to be effective, he or she must be under the guidance of a spiritual mentor.

The church was divinely commissioned to "make disciples." This means to make every convert into a learner and then a teacher. How can we fulfill our mission if we aren't properly and adequately informed in matters of the scriptures? This should encourage every man of God to be a constant student of the word of God.

Is Bible College Training Important?

I strongly believe in pursuing not only general education but also higher education. People called to be in the ministry must put a premium on having a college degree or academic training. They must use the faculties God has given them and never put them to waste. They should learn to organize their thoughts, develop critical thinking, discriminate or discern, and organize and systematize. These will help a church leader be at par with the world in the field of science and literature. We ought not to take a back seat and compromise our academic standards in the name of faith. We should accomplish this goal by attending a college or university with full accreditation.

However, when it comes to the things of God and the ministry, the training must be done through the agency of the local church. The Lord made this point apparently clear in the last part of the commission found in Matthew 28:20. "Teaching them to observe all things whatsoever I have commanded you."

My answer, therefore, to the particular question "Is Bible College training important?" is a resounding no.

Let me explain. In the scriptures, the effective training approach wasn't group instructions but a one-on-one teaching approach or personal mentoring. In the Old Testament, Moses mentored Joshua, and Elijah worked closely with Elisha. In the New Testament, Jesus trained the apostles; Paul was under Ananias, and when he was young, he was under the feet of Gamaliel; Paul mentored Timothy. They were trained not by educational institutions but by trainers and mentors within a certain locality.

This personal mentoring approach is no longer widely practiced in most churches today. Let me give some reasons:

1. Pastors have become too busy to train leaders. As a result, they relinquish the training responsibility to professional teachers.
2. Churches don't have an effective system to provide training.
3. Church members aren't supportive of this because they want their leaders to spend more time ministering to them.
4. Some pastors aren't comfortable training somebody who might usurp their authority and grab their position in the future. The idea of losing their job intimidates them.
5. Pastors simply fail to train leaders. They only train people to be followers.
6. Churches are more focused on building their membership than on training and building leaders with character.
7. The work of the ministry has become a profession rather than a calling.

Churches will never lack preachers, and workers today will be better served and equipped with capable leaders and Christian workers if pastors would only take the time and responsibility through mentoring.

The need for an independent Bible college stemmed from the failure of churches and leaders to train, as explained previously. Because of this, for most pastors, when one surrendered to the ministry, the first order of events was to send him to a Bible college. Unfortunately, Bible colleges, though sufficiently funded and operated, cannot and will never take the place of a local church and a local pastor in training a new preacher. A local church has a certain uniqueness not found in Bible colleges. This uniqueness is important in allowing the student to understand the ministry in a greater and meaningful way.

This doesn't mean, however, that all Bible colleges are doing things wrong. A few of those remaining under the authority of the local church do things right. This author, however, doesn't support a teaching ministry or Bible college that is outside the authority and jurisdiction of a local assembly.

As a matter of preference and as the senior pastor of the International Bible Baptist Church, I have made the decision not to allow others to train our preachers. I personally take my mentoring job seriously. All preachers and future leaders in the ministry of our church will need to receive firsthand training from me as their senior pastor. It is the responsibility of every pastor to personally train and mentor every leader in the church. I face my position seriously as a pastor and teacher. Every pastor must do the same.

The following are the risks of allowing others to train your preachers and leaders:

1. You lose the bright, talented, and motivated workers to another church with a Bible college program.
2. Young people who surrender to the ministry with the intent to serve in their local churches end up serving in another ministry after being offered better opportunities and salaries.
3. The loyalty toward the pastor who sends them and the church that prays and supports them is diverted to the pastors and churches hosting and operating the school.
4. Preachers always tend to respect those people who train them. If others train your workers, you won't get their loyalty.
5. Some students, when they come back home from Bible college, think they know better than their pastor does. Pride can destroy a church worker and potentially destroy a church.
6. Students can learn things that may be contrary to the ideals and practices of your local church. The result can be devastating.
7. The pioneering spirit is lost because preachers who are away from their churches lose the opportunity of seeing the actual development of their church and the sacrifices of their people.
8. Professional teachers who have limited knowledge or lack pastoral or ministerial experiences teach the young student preachers.

For those pastors or churches who are ill equipped to provide appropriate training, there are few Bible colleges out there that are doing their best, by God's grace. You can avail yourself of their program. However, some guidelines must be established:

1. The Bible college must be under the authority of a local church that has the same convictions you do.
2. Teachers or instructors must be active in pastoral ministry or any other related ministry.
3. Students must come home and serve in your local church during weekends, holidays, summer vacation, and other times when they are out of school.
4. Students must be instructed that they need to put their local church on the top of the list when they consider future service, employment, and opportunities in the ministry.
5. The church must keep track of the developments, changes, and status of the school or the church that operates the school. You may not be aware of a new pastor; hence there may be a new emphasis and orientation.
6. It must be the course of action for the pastor and church to communicate with the students regularly and pray for them. This step makes students realize they are being missed.
7. Send your students to school with your ministry in their minds. You can do so by constantly communicating with them through personal correspondence, phone calls, e-mails, and personal visits.

Bible Institute

Another tried and effective way of approaching this need is to develop a Bible institute program. This program allows students to learn the Bible from a mentor, the pastor of the local church. It also allows students to see firsthand how the systems work. It is an on-the-job training experience.

To start a Bible institute, you need to develop curriculum based on your local church distinctive. There is no need to get accreditation to start. A dedicated facility also isn't needed to operate it. A Bible institute program will provide your students with formal lessons and the moral confidence that they are receiving serious and legitimate training. As the pastor, you need to be the administrator or head instructor. Be sure you know how to begin, lead, teach, and maintain this program.

Again, while you teach your people the things of God and how to serve Him right, encourage them to get a degree in basic sciences such as languages, math, social sciences, and other courses that will help them in communicating the truth effectively. With this, they will become more well rounded and capable individuals. Allow them to pursue a degree and apply their learned skills through a vocation that will complement the ministry.

Most people have more respect and consideration for those who have academic credentials. It's important for some people to see what leaders are capable of doing. Remember, men look at the outward appearance. Allowing them to work outside the church setting provides them the exposure of what it's like to be in the world system. It also allows them to interact with people they want to reach with the gospel. This experience will help them get regularly informed of what is going on outside the church (for example, new developments and trends that need to be addressed or challenged according to the word of God). This will also send a message that our preachers, though living by the gospel, are faced with the same needs as anybody in this world.

Continuing Education and Training

Another area that needs to be seriously considered in the ministry of church planting is the necessity of ongoing training of preachers and staff—training the pastor administers and supervises under the local church.

Many preachers become disillusioned with the ministry due to their lack of understanding of current trends and pressing issues. This lack of understanding causes church workers to be unprepared to face the daily challenges in life, thus rendering them ineffective in the ministry.

No wonder most fundamental churches have lost the dynamism and have run out of better ideas so that workers have begun to look for a better training ground to enhance their abilities and effectiveness. This issue started the rise and popularity of leadership conferences and seminars, replacing the training that has been lacking in many churches today.

Unfortunately, many pastors aren't able to relate with most of the materials and the kind of training they receive since they don't have access to the same resources and opportunities. They are lured to attend because they need the sense of hope.

The mega-church ministry hosting the conference has all the impressive qualities of a successful church ministry: beautiful buildings, impressive architectural design, stately halls and auditoriums, impressive guest speakers, and extravagant promotions. They seem so powerful in enticing pastors and preachers from small congregations to attend. They become the captive audience for several days or weeks, totally submerged in the belief that if they follow the principles they receive during the conference, they will see the same results in their ministry. These results constitute success in the ministry, so they say.

Success has been redefined to mean being big and great. It has been perceived as "Do what our church does, and you would be successful." No longer is it "Do what the Bible tells you to do."

If the Lord Jesus Christ had gone through the same standard of scrutiny these mega churches go through today, He would surely have been deemed unsuccessful, perhaps even a failure. He saw multitudes get saved during His earthly ministry, yet we find Him working with only a handful of people at all times. He was practically by Himself when He died on the cross. Most of the apostles abandoned Him except John the Beloved.

Preachers today have been conditioned to view success unrealistically. No wonder they get frustrated and disappointed when they go back to their local churches after the conference at the mega church. They are again confronted with the reality that they don't have the same resources the mega churches do. The facility is small, people are few, resources are limited, and there is no money in the bank. The good feelings last for only a week or a season. Most of the things they learned are also found inapplicable and impractical in real-case scenarios. The purchased workbooks and manuals occupy the too-common location: bookshelves soon to be invaded by cobwebs.

To solve the distressing feeling of frustration, pastors and churches must devise a system to allow their church workers to connect with current trends and new challenges in the ministry. They need to take relevant courses and explore other approaches to be more effective. Sometimes doing so can result in compromising the foundation and landmarks of faith. To some this is the only way to make the principles of God and His word relevant to our day and to the lives of the local church members.

An ongoing approach in training and education for our preachers and leaders is the final answer to this need. For the International Bible Baptist Church, our intention is to provide this opportunity and require all preachers and pastors to undergo a continuing education program to maintain their effectiveness. If other professions require their members to go through continuing education to maintain their license, why think less of the ministry? The Lord's work is more important because it can provide greater help and encouragement to the people. This truth must behoove us to be greatly responsible for the glory of God.

Chapter 4
THE ROLE OF THE PASTOR'S FAMILY

Pioneering a ministry is the most challenging task in all Christian service. Only a few people can qualify in this league. With God's grace, proper training, and understanding of the work of the church planter, any God-called man can certainly do the job. Pioneers face some difficulties not found in any spiritual vocation or calling. Often they do feel alone, and the only visible people they can count on for trust and support are their immediate family. Praise God for the promise He has given in Hebrews 13:5. "I will never leave thee nor forsake thee." Matthew says 28:20, "And lo I am with you always." Both verses provide a guarantee of God's eternal presence in the ministry.

No wonder the apostle Paul, in giving the qualification of a bishop in 1 Timothy 3:2 and Titus 1:6, stated that a "bishop must be a husband of one wife." This instruction doesn't at all discriminate against single pastors or preachers. I believe the beloved apostle, based on his experience of being single, knew loneliness in the ministry. He encouraged all those called in the ministry to find a wife to serve with them. It's ideal for men who seek to serve God in a pastoral capacity to be married.

I don't claim to be an expert in family relationships and affairs, but I have experienced enough challenges in life that have given me more than enough reasons to share with you some few thoughts and ideas in this primer. Let me approach this by explaining the individual role of every member of the pastor's family.

The Pastor, the Husband, the Father

A pastor's role shouldn't clash with his role as a husband and father. Instead, these roles must complement one another. To avoid a clash, the roles must not only be clearly defined but also be conscientiously and carefully carried out. The change of roles demands a skill in leadership and multitasking.

People who occupy different roles feel like they juggle themselves into different positions while facing various tasks. I'm not sure whether the term "juggle" can fully describe the change of roles. I want to think of it the complementary roles of pastor, husband and father as entering into another door of opportunity, like entering another door within the same house to face a different kind of demand and expectations. It isn't random, but it is a deliberate decision to move and perform a particular role or behavior in different settings. This kind of perspective will not only help us accept the multitasking responsibility. It will also command respect to the roles we are facing.

Defining your roles will help avoid overlapping and getting confused with the positions you occupy. While you can be a godly and loving husband to your wife and a wonderful father to your children at home, in church you can still be a caring pastor *and* the responsible administrator of a Christian school.

To do so, it is important that you don't bring your church role home with you. As a father, maintain familial and intimate relationships with your wife and children when you are at home. Model the life of Christ to them without treating them as church members at home and "pastoring" them.

In the church, instruct them to take the role as members. That way they understand that they are responsible only to God, being the head of the church. Your family needs to respect you as the pastor and must similarly address you as the same. This will show church members that everybody is equal before God. This truth should be projected to all people in the church.

This doesn't mean, however, that your family ceases to be a family unit in church. It's still a family, but it must not take precedence over the responsibility a pastor has to God. In the church, your immediate family is *not* your primary responsibility; it is the work of God.

As a pastor, you occupy several tasks: that of a pastor, teacher, husband, father, administrator, counselor, youth leader, citizen, and law enforcer, among others. Each role is important and requires different leadership skills. Do each role accordingly through God's power and grace.

The Pastor's Wife

The role of the pastor's wife is unique. While she addresses her husband as "pastor" in the church, she must continue her role as a loving and supportive wife to the man of God. Members need to see that relationship. The strong marital relationship of the pastor and his wife is a good testimony of a working relationship.

The "pastor's wife" isn't a defined position in the church. It isn't a position of responsibility provided in the scriptures. You don't find any preacher's wife in the Bible occupying a position of responsibility in the New Testament church. The office of a pastor is complex enough to include the wife in the church staff. However, if the pastor's wife needs to occupy a position in the ministry, the position must be one that complements her husband.

The pastor's wife can find herself in a difficult situation due to people's expectations. This happens when church members don't fully understand her role. As previously stated, the role of a pastor's wife isn't an office the scriptures provide; therefore, the church must not place any expectations on her. Her husband, who is the pastor, is the one who sets these on her.

Assigning the wife to a leadership position equal to that of the pastoral staff is *not* a wise and appropriate decision. She must not be placed in a level of responsibility similar or equal to that of the assistant pastors. Even without a leadership position in a church, the pastor's wife is a respected role. It carries an aura of God-given respect for her willingness to minister to God's chosen man. It carries respect from all the members of the church because of her association with the leader, the husband, the man of God. When a pastor's wife occupies a strong leadership position in a church, this can be stressful to the marital relationship and polarize the family and church.

In the church, the pastor's wife should maintain a close motherly relationship with her children. They need to have a parent who is physically present with them in the church at all times. The emotional nurture, together with the mother's physical presence, is very important to the self-esteem of the pastor's kids. If both parents are busy with the affairs of the church, the kids will feel neglected and abandoned. The role of the pastor's wife is to provide their children with emotional nurture and parental presence so that they won't feel neglected or abandoned.

The pastor occupies a very significant and demanding position, and too often he won't find time to meet the needs of his own children. A godly wife fulfills these needs and provides understanding of the emotional yearnings of the kids. The responsibility of the pastor's wife is to protect, uphold, respect, and explain the duties of her husband to the children. She must not use the absence of the pastor or father to promote herself as a martyr or a hero for the children by stating that their father has no time for them.

If there are no children at home, the pastor's wife must focus on her job as a helpmeet. Her ministry is the pastor, and she must take care of his physical and emotional needs. God has brought her in his life to make things easy for him, to fulfill his duty and calling as a pastor without any hindrance. In the same way, God has brought the pastor into her life to fulfill her desire to serve her loving God.

The loving wife of a pastor helps her husband function properly in the church. She provides physical nourishment, comfort, and whatever else is needed for her husband to perform his duty as the man of God. If she needs to engage in church ministry, this role should complement the pastor and must be under his personal direction. The wife must not find herself being pulled in different directions because she needs to meet the needs of her husband alongside the demands of the ministry she engages in. The priority of the pastor's wife is always her husband.

It's vitally important for the whole church to understand the role of the preacher's wife to avoid misunderstandings.

The Pastor's Kids

The pastor's kids or PKs, as they are called, are in a culture of their own as they cope with the demands of being so. Growing up as a PK wasn't easy for me because of the high expectations church members placed on my two brothers and me. Because our father was the associate pastor, we felt like we were in a glass house; we were daily scrutinized, observed, and judged. While we enjoyed the fame and popularity, we also resented the idea that we had to act and move a certain way to give the ministry a good name. We were everybody's children, and we got everybody's attention, good and bad. They all sounded and appeared good, but there was a dear price to pay: our privacy and the loss of our individuality.

Preachers' kids haven't chosen their position in life. They are placed in the ring of responsibility because of their father's calling to the ministry. Their experiences don't need to be negative or traumatic. The negative experience can be easily avoided if the pastor and his wife are properly oriented regarding proper parenting of their special children.

The preacher's children have special needs that are totally different from those of other children; hence they are special children. The burden of responsibility is on parents, who are supposed to train them. One of these responsibilities is to protect them from the scrutiny of church members. This is done by simply explaining their children's position in the ministry. The following are some practical tips:

1. Understand that when the pastor's kids are in church, they don't have a special position and shouldn't receive special treatment. They need to be treated like everyone else. Encourage them to address you as "pastor" or "preacher."
2. Let the mother be the parent figure to supervise the children in church at all times. They need to relate with the rest of the

children who have parents in the church by also enjoying a family that prays and worships God together.

3. Let the children understand that they aren't obligated to serve or occupy a position of responsibility just because their father is the pastor of the church. If they need to be involved, this should be because they have felt the Spirit of God convicting them accordingly.

4. The pastor must not play the role of the Holy Spirit by demanding that his children serve God when it is against their will to do so. It's important that the kids have a positive church experience.

5. Allow the pastor's kids to be children.

6. The pastor must clearly explain to the children their position in the church.

7. The pastor must be consistent in his behavior at home and in the church. The kids observe him all the time.

The Pastor's Extended Family

Since our ministry is multiethnic, addressing this issue is important since it is unique in some cultures, especially among Asians, Hispanics, and Africans. The presence of extended family members can cause some difficulties in the life of the minister if this matter isn't appropriately addressed. This practice goes back to the Old Testament when God assigned the whole tribe of Levi to handle the work in the temple as priests. The Jews dealt not only with the man of God but also with a whole tribe chosen with the task of ministering as priests in the temple of God.

In other cultures, some perceive that a ministry is considered a "family" calling. This thinking gives the notion that the pastor's relatives are given the same rights and privileges as the pastor. This perception has complicated the role of the pastor and confused the minds of the members. In this case, the calling is no longer of the Lord but of the family. This is seen in the pastoral succession; some expect the next son in line to succeed in the pastoral responsibility without having received the calling of the Lord.

In the New Testament economy, calling is individual and personal. While everybody is called to win souls, each individual must respond personally to the special call of God. One isn't called based on family affiliation or relationship. The pastor must not favor members of his family just because they carry the same last name. Extended family members must be treated as equal to all members of the church.

Chapter 5
STARTING A NEW TESTAMENT CHURCH

When I started the International Bible Baptist Ministry, I was a one-man band. I was the preacher, teacher, song leader, pianist, visitation worker, and custodian who prepared the church facility for the worship service. It wasn't an easy start. I began this pioneering work with only the help of my sending church, Bible Baptist Church of Marysville, California, which supported me with a total of $120 per month for one year. It was only through God's grace that I survived the trials and difficulties of a pioneering work.

Now that we have a parent organization alongside other ministries (Association of International Bible Baptist Churches; Asia-Pacific Independent Baptist Fellowship; Metropolitan, International, and Lighthouse Endeavors), International Bible Baptist Church planters don't need to experience the same difficulty I went through. They now have a church and experienced leaders who can guide them through the difficult process. They have a model to follow, able workers to work with, and a very supportive church to count on. There is no reason for any church planter under the ministry of IBBC to fail because of the strong support, training, and readily available resources.

Outreach and mission preachers can always get the assistance of any IBBC preachers to help in any way, whether in preaching, teaching, visiting, counseling, and so forth. This help, however, isn't intended to be permanent. We cannot allow church planters to permanently use workers from the mother church or from other affiliated congregations to assist their ministry. The assistance extended to preachers is designed to assist them during the initial process in the development of the ministry and initially to help train local people to serve God.

The true asset of any church is people: the individuals you need to evangelize and train. Without them, there is no justification for the programs, buildings, or finances in the church. The ministry begins and ends with people. This is the major thrust of IBBC, as mentioned in our motto "The Church with a Heart for Souls."

To help understand the needs of people, a church planter must understand where they come from, what their needs are, and where they fit in the ministry. In doing so, it's best to categorize them as they come in. This strategy will help in the church's stability.

For this reason, the ministry of International Bible Baptist Church has devised a way to categorize the members who come in. To maintain its effectiveness and sustain the growth of the church, a certain ratio must be maintained.

Membership Categories

A safe and reachable membership ratio will secure the growth and stability in the ministry. This is important since many church planters and preachers today count more on transfers or people coming in as members from other churches.

While the influx of people from other churches can be numerically attractive, you need to remember that these people were trained and taught differently. There can be an adverse complication in the long run. To secure a safe and reachable membership ratio, I have developed a way to categorize every member of the church through generational fields to help monitor and determine the membership makeup of a church.

- First generational field: These people are immediately saved and baptized in the local church directly under the pastor's ministry.

These are also the members who are directly saved and baptized in your outreaches, satellites, and/or mission congregations.

- Second generational field: These people are saved in other churches or ministries but baptized in your ministry, including those who are considered "rebaptized."
- Third generational field: These people transfer from another church by means of statement and letter, but they have given their allegiance and loyalty to your local church.

It's important that the ratio of the first generational field remain higher than the other generational fields. To accomplish this, it is vital for your church to concentrate more in the ministry of soul winning to see more people saved and baptized locally. The ideal percentage of the first generation members must be 70 percent and higher. The people who are saved and baptized in your ministry will consist of the most faithful and loyal members of your congregation. These are those you personally and spiritually raised and trained. They see how you work, and they have observed you closely in your sacrifices for the ministry. They practically grow with you and learn from you. They are the people who will stand beside you and behind you through thick and thin.

The second generational field members have great potential as long as they are solidly oriented with the policies, doctrines, and practices of the local church. These people can come out as loyal and faithful as the first generation members. They confirm in their hearts the power and reality of their newfound faith.

Generally, the third generational group has a lower percentage of people who come out committed to the work of the Lord. However, those who are really faithful and committed, no matter how few, will be your most loyal leaders and members. However, you will find in this group a greater percentage of people who may also be opportunistic; if given a chance, they will pursue personal ambition and cause problems in the church. While some join your church with a noble reason, others join your church out of curiosity and the desire to prove to their former church that they can succeed in another church. Most merely want to escape from a problematic church relationship.

Reaching Out to People Groups

Another area that needs important consideration in the ministry is the racial makeup of the mission or congregation. By racial makeup, I mean the people you are targeting to reach with the gospel. When asked to explain why they are in the ministry, most preachers give a generic answer, such as "to serve the Lord," "to win some souls," or "to start a church." I learned from experience that when we express our goals or objectives, they should be simple, direct, clear, measurable, and focused. The Bible gives a good example of clearly stated objectives. Consider the following:

1. "Go ye into all the world." This means all; no place or people are left unreached with the gospel (Mark 16:15).
2. "Ye shall be witnesses unto me both in Jerusalem, and in all Judaea, and in Samaria, and unto the uttermost part of the earth." This has the idea of simultaneous evangelism that touches all people groups all over the world (Acts 1:8).
3. The apostle Paul said at one time, "My heart's desire and prayer to God for Israel is, that they might be saved." Paul's goal was focused, and that was to reach Israel (Rom. 10:1). These are just some examples we can gather from the Bible. The Lord wants us to be clear in our objectives. In the scriptures, we are clearly mandated to reach all people groups. Acts 1:8 says, "But ye shall receive power, after that the Holy Ghost is come upon you: and ye shall be witnesses unto me both in Jerusalem, and in all Judaea, and in Samaria, and unto the uttermost part of the earth."

The above passage specifically states that our desire must be to reach not only the people we know but also others we don't know. Jesus told us to reach simultaneously or at the same time the following:

- "Jerusalem": this refers to the people we know and are closely familiar and acquainted with.
- "Judea": this refers to our neighbors or people other than those we know closely.

- "Samaria": this refers to the people who don't like us, those who avoid us, and those whom we don't like and avoid.
- "Unto the uttermost": this refers to people who are not easily reached with the gospel, such as those in another country or continent.

To fulfill this mandate, a church needs to devise a system or plan to be constantly aware of the people living in a given community.

First, study the demographics of the community. This is the study of human population, which includes the size, growth, distribution, and racial makeup of the people living in the community. This information can be easily retrieved from the Internet. Knowing the kind of people living in a community will help the congregation target these people effectively.

Second, map out the community by indicating the different concentrations of people groups.

Third, saturate the community by using appropriate materials to reach these people groups. Use a survey form to identify the language and needs of the population. Include a worker's evaluation form, an assessment form a church worker uses to evaluate the people in the community.

Fourth, do follow-up work on individuals who express interest during the survey by using church workers who are culturally sensitive and appropriately prepared (age and gender) to reach the different people groups. Have a culture-sensitivity training program for all workers in the church.

Begin this system by doing the same with all the members of your congregation. In the survey form, ask members to identify the people group they belong to and the languages they speak. In the evaluation form, ask church workers to identify the people they can reach with the gospel. This system will provide a cultural sensitivity, diversity, and multiethnic approach to the ministry. To attain the goals in evangelism, the local church needs to deliberately reach all the people groups with the gospel of the Lord within a given community.

The Church as a Service Organization

Most churches today are only in the business to gather people or numbers. Even the ministry can be reduced to a number game. The same is true with most people. They act as merely consumers of religion. They attend to enjoy the benefits of membership. They are entertained and served. Their "offerings or financial giving" to the church becomes a fee for spiritual services such as entertainment, comfort, entertainment, and the support group they cannot find elsewhere. Pastors and churches have been reduced to service providers, entertainers, motivational speakers, and counselors, among other things. The members are mostly takers, not givers. Most churchgoers are not involved in the ministry.

The Bible plainly states in Ephesians 2:10 that God has saved us to "be His workmanship created in Christ Jesus unto good works." God's desire is for His church to train and teach people so they can serve. That is the true essence of discipleship.

God designed churches this way so that churches can continually have workers and evangelists to preach and teach the whole counsel of God. Members not involved in the ministry of service aren't doing the will of God. We're supposed to minister like the Lord Jesus Christ who "came not to be ministered unto but to minister and to give His life a ransom for many" (Mark 10:46). The book of Mark describes Him as the servant of God.

Ephesians 4:1–16 states the true nature and character of the church. "I therefore, the prisoner of the Lord, beseech you that ye walk worthy of the vocation wherewith ye are called, With all lowliness and meekness, with longsuffering, forbearing one another in love; Endeavouring to keep the unity of the Spirit in the bond of peace. There is one body, and one Spirit, even as ye are called in one hope of your calling; One Lord, one faith, one baptism, One God and Father of all, who is above all, and through all, and in you all."

The passage begins with an encouragement to the members of the church of Ephesus to "walk worthy of the vocation wherewith ye are called." The word *vocation* is defined as a calling, course of action, occupation, or special function. It infers that every member of a local church must be engaged in a particular function to benefit the whole body. The apostle Paul, as he continued to instruct the church in Ephesus, enumerated seven reasons why all members must unite to fulfill the work of the Lord:

1. One body: we belong to a church in a particular locality where we ought to function and serve.
2. One Spirit: the same Spirit inspires and empowers us.
3. One hope: we preach the same hope of eternal glory and opportunity.
4. One Lord: we have the same Master, one Commander-in-Chief, who is the Lord Jesus Christ.
5. One faith: we have one book, the source of our only faith and practice.
6. One baptism: we are one in our first act of obedience (in other words, the waters of baptism).
7. One God and Father of all: we worship the same God of the Bible.

The purpose of unity is for all members of the local church to focus on building each other up to be effective witnesses of the gospel of the Lord Jesus Christ as a whole body. A member who is of no service to the Lord in a local church isn't living in obedience to God's will. It is therefore the responsibility of the church to teach, equip, and train every member to serve and glorify God. Ephesians 4:16 says, "From whom the whole body fitly joined together and compacted by that which every joint supplieth, according to the effectual working in the measure of every part, maketh increase of the body unto the edifying of itself in love."

The Church with a Heart for Souls

International Bible Baptist Church (IBBC) Theme Song
By Hernes M. Abante
October 9, 1998

From the Bible we read Jesus Christ as He led.
He had gathered those whom He saved
And began His great church
To proclaim the great word.
He had called them to take up His cause.

Chorus:

We're a church with a great heart for souls
Set apart to reach the untold.
Let's go out to the lost
And bring them to the cross.
We're a church with a great heart for souls.
(Repeat chorus to end after verse 2.)

We're a part of the flock, the great people of God.
Our message is "Jesus saves."
Share His gospel to all.
Baptize them to the fold
And to teach them to follow His plan.
(Go to chorus.)

Chapter 6
THE CHURCH AS A LEADERSHIP TRAINING INSTITUTION

God mandated the New Testament church to be a training institution. No other institution has been chosen to train godly men of God. This mandate wasn't given to any educational institution—not to the government, not to a world organization such as the United Nations, and not even to a particular religion or denomination. This mandate was given only to the local New Testament church.

Since the responsibility of teaching and training individuals was given to the local church, it is important for the pastor to have the leadership skills and resources for training others. The church must develop a training program for all ages. Every single member of the local church must go through a training process, for God intends all believers to be His servants and faithful workers. The following are some practical ways to train people for the divine tasks:

Train Your Members to Be Leaders

Second Timothy 2:2 says, "And the things that thou hast heard of me among many witnesses, the same commit thou to faithful men, who shall be able to teach others also." Most leaders train, but not all people they train are trained as leaders. We need to train all our members to be potential leaders today and in the future. Many pastors find it difficult to start the process of training leaders because they haven't caught the idea that a spiritual leader is a leader of leaders. Typically, leaders lead because of personal ambition and desire. Others have reached their leadership position by going through the ranks. Others acquire the position through natural ascendency.

Training leaders must be a deliberate move. It must occupy an important part in the program of the church. This begins by having the new members fill out a membership evaluation and assessment form to state their personal information, including interests, talents, plans, vision, and what they feel the will of God is in their lives. With this information, you can know their desires and inclinations and in what area of service they can fit in. The most important area isn't what abilities or talents they have but God's will in their lives.

God's way isn't to depend on man's wisdom and abilities. Everybody, even the person who is an expert in his or her field, must go through a spiritual training process. This training is to build character and discipline to do the job right until he or she has developed the character of Christ.

First Corinthians 1:26–29 says, "For ye see your calling, brethren, how that not many wise men after the flesh, not many mighty, not many noble, are called: But God hath chosen the foolish things of the world to confound the wise; and God hath chosen the weak things of the world to confound the things which are mighty; And base things of the world, and things which are despised, hath God chosen, yea, and things which are not, to bring to nought things that are: That no flesh should glory in his presence."

The pastor must look not at the abilities of people but at the potential they have when the Lord begins to work in their lives. This doesn't mean to put to waste what they know and can do in the ministry. Their abilities, if they really have them, must first be surrendered to God before they can be used in the ministry of the Lord.

When the pastor looks at the potential of the individual, he considers what the Lord can do in his or her life, not what a man or woman can do. Looking for potential is a process by which a local church taps into or exposes the gifts and talents the Lord has given him or her by means of training and exposure in the ministry.

This is important because so many churches are desperate for people with talents. What usually happens is that church leaders advertise the need such as music or teaching, and those who fit and are considered experts in the field get the job purely on the basis of personal merit and abilities. This promotion can result in pride and arrogance, since these people know they are needed in the ministry. However, when looking at the potential, a leader can discover the person's inclination (music and teaching), and with this, a training process can begin. This is God's grace in the area of serving. Service in the local church is a privilege.

Train Them Young: "Train Up a Child"

Proverbs 22:6 says, "Train up a child in the way he should go: and when he is old, he will not depart from it." Training must begin early while the child is still pliable and willing. While training begins at home with parental supervision, it must not stop there. The church has a responsibility to train a young child to be a faithful follower of the Lord Jesus Christ. This training must ideally be done through the family—it means training the parents to raise the children on God's foundation. Somebody said a child must be trained years before he or she is born. Proper training of a child starts with the mom and dad before they become parents.

The local church is in a strategic position to provide training not only because it has a divine mandate but also because of Sunday school and other children's programs. Through kids' programs and lessons, children can learn obedience, responsibility, honesty, and other precious nuggets to get them ready for maturity and independence.

Children can be developed into future leaders by exposing them to leadership activities at a tender age. The junior church program is a great and wonderful example in providing this kind of exposure to our kids using the different ministries in the church. Through this program, they are able to participate in the ministry of giving, ushering, song leading, announcing, teaching, and even preaching at a tender age. These activities will help them learn to serve and appreciate the different opportunities for service in the local church.

Having the goal of training leaders in their tender ages would provide greater motivation to the members of the church. This makes a powerful statement that the ministry or the work of the Lord is available to all. Anyone in the local church, as long as he or she is available and willing, can serve the Lord and enjoy the blessings such ministry offers.

Teach Them the "Whole Counsel of God"

Matthew 28:20 says, "Teaching them to observe all things whatsoever I have commanded you." The word of God is written for all believers. Unbelievers can never understand the scriptures for they are "foolishness" to them. One needs to have spiritual discernment to comprehend the message of the Bible. Only people the Holy Spirit indwelt can truly claim and practice what the Bible declares, and they are the only ones who can learn, proclaim, and practice the word of God.

The goal of every local church must be to teach all its members everything the Bible declares. There is no double standard when it comes to the communication of divine truth. The only limitation is the readiness of the believer, which is totally dependent on his or her level of maturity. As 1 Peter 2:2 states, the baby in Christ is given the milk of God's word. However, the Bible also states that the mature believer must partake of the meat of God's word.

> Therefore leaving the principles of the doctrine of Christ, let us go on unto perfection; not laying again the foundation of repentance from dead works, and of faith toward God, Of the doctrine of baptisms, and of laying on of hands, and of resurrection of the dead, and of eternal judgment. (Heb. 6:1–2)

> But grow in grace, and in the knowledge of our Lord and Saviour Jesus Christ. To him be glory both now and for ever. Amen. (2 Peter 3:18)

The only qualification needed in believers is obedience in the waters of baptism after they receive the Lord. An obedient child of God is willing to be taught the word of God. Notice the logical arrangement of the commission as stated: get people saved first and then baptized before teaching them. It would be futile to teach a disobedient and uncommitted believer the whole counsel of God.

Teach Them by Example

James 1:22 says, "But be ye doers of the word, and not hearers only, deceiving your own selves." The word of God is a living word. Since it is alive, it is therefore dynamic and powerful. The author of the book of Hebrews describes it as "quick, and powerful, and sharper than any two-edged sword, piercing even to the dividing asunder of soul and spirit, and of the joints and marrow" (Heb. 4:12)

God's word isn't a collection of principles or set of rules that should remain only in the pages of the holy book. It must be translated and written in our hearts. We need to encourage members of the local church to commit God's word to practice. We must present the Bible in the most practical sense, making every word relevant to our day and time.

"Modeling" is an effective teaching approach. It is teaching life through righteous behavior and practical service. It is teaching by doing. It goes hand in hand with "mentoring," a one-on-one teaching approach. We shouldn't follow Lao Tzu, an old Chinese sage who said, "Don't do what I do, but do what I say." As preachers and teachers of the words of God, let us not only be announcers or declarers of the truth but also be doers, showing the works and beauty of the Savior in us.

Teach Them to Completion

Second Timothy 3:17 says, "That the man of God may be perfect, throughly furnished unto all good works." The final goal of teaching is to make the man of God "perfect" or complete. Being perfect doesn't mean becoming holy like God and sinless. It means being mature and ready to serve and teach others. The apostle Paul stated that some "ought to be teachers" and not remain in the rudiments of Christianity. The only way believers may know whether they have learned is the ability to duplicate their lives in another. Second Timothy 2:2 encourages us to commit to others all the things we have learned and heard. "And the things that thou hast heard of me among many witnesses, the same commit thou to faithful men, who shall be able to teach others also."

If the local church is focused on training leaders, there won't be any shortage of workers in the church. The church will have an ample pool of qualified people to do the job. Since they have been trained, they can be called on to serve in any capacity the Lord wants them to. There must be someone in the local church who is willing and able to fill any position, including the office of the pastor if a tragedy or major problem occurs.

The best growth is from within. Anybody who is hired to occupy a position is considered a "hireling" in the minds of some people. However, if leaders are taken from the same body of believers, the level of confidence is greater, and the transition is less stressful because of greater familiarity with the chosen leaders. Even in medical science, anything that comes from the outside is considered a foreign matter, and rejection will likely occur.

Chapter 7
DEVELOPMENT OF A CONGREGATION

God is interested in a growing and progressive relationship. He wants to see commitment, dedication, and service in all His creation. He established a home to see the family work, grow, and propagate together. Relationships are also the goal of redemption. The Lord Jesus Christ died to allow us to have a personal relationship with God as the Father. He also expects us to grow in this relationship.

The purpose of the church is one and the same. The Lord Jesus established it in order for this relationship to grow. The church is the spiritual home where His children can be nurtured, fed, trained, equipped for the ministry, and sent out to multiply. Soul winning leads to church planting. The two must never be divorced. You need to have a spiritual home for people who are saved. Church planting, therefore, carries the idea of relationship—a spiritual relationship, that is.

Similar to a family, for a congregation to start, a mother church must give birth to it. Just like a mother, a church that gives birth to another church allows not only the birth but also the sustenance, support, and most importantly, its procreation and authority. This church then becomes a legitimate body. Eventually, this young congregation will become an independent church, which can start another cycle of church life.

When the Holy Spirit empowered the New Testament church, as revealed in Acts 2, the Lord promised its perpetuity and continuity. This means the empowered church will always have its presence in every generation until His second coming. This promise of continuity was declared after He organized His church during His personal earthly ministry.

Matthew 16:18 says, "I will build my Church and the gates of hell shall not prevail against it." This wasn't the promise of the founding of the church. He had already established the church when he gathered the apostles and disciples during His time. He referred to the building of the church, which began on the day of Pentecost. The Lord had in His mind the idea of reaching the world with the gospel. The church will continue to be built all over the world until He comes.

In Matthew 16:18, the Lord talked to Peter, not to appoint him as the founder of the church or the first pope but to use him in the inaugural worldwide ministry of the church of the living God. True enough, the weak and opinionated Peter became the bold preacher after the empowerment that was instrumental in the salvation of over three thousand souls. The souls that were saved came from different nations—a fulfillment of Acts 1:8 as evident by the miracle of tongues.

God gave authority to the church to prevail and continue in all generations when He said, " And the gates of hell shall not prevail against it." The promise of perpetuity began on the day of Pentecost with the 120 members who were faithful enough and committed to wait for the Holy Spirit.

To illustrate church authority, we find in Acts 8 that Deacon Philip went to Samaria to preach, and many souls were saved, including Simon the Sorcerer. After the converts were baptized, the church in Jerusalem—the empowered church—heard of the results in Samaria. They sent Peter and John, and we find that they laid their hands on the converts so they would receive the Holy Spirit.

Since the converts saved under Philip were already Spirit indwelt and baptized with the baptism of John, what was the purpose of the laying on of hands? The purpose was to provide unction and authority for the converts in Samaria to be established as a New Testament church. It was a mother church giving birth to another. It was a mother church giving another life to a church to exist and continue the works of the Lord.

"Laying on of hands" speaks of approval and authority. No church can ever start and exist without a mother church providing the authority to exist. Every church must have a link to another independent church. That is the essence of Matthew 16:18. That is the purpose of the empowerment. This shows that God is a God of order and decency. He provides a pattern in the ministry for us to follow and maintain.

To have a divine and legitimate assembly, you need to be sure you belong to an empowered church, one with proper authority and linked to the promise in Matthew 16:18. What use would a promise be if there was no truth to it?

The following gives to us the progression in the development of a congregation.

Home Bible Study Groups (Cell Groups)

A home Bible study (HBS) is the most effective way to start a congregation. Church members and leaders must be encouraged to start many HBS groups in some key locations within the local church community. Its aim is to reach the people who normally wouldn't visit a church but would be willing to go to a home. This is the initial obedience to the "go" command.

Acts 5:42 says, "And daily in the temple, and in every house, they ceased not to teach and preach Jesus Christ." The purpose of the HBS is to win the souls of those in the community. People are strongly encouraged to bring unsaved people from the neighborhood. HBS serves to teach, encourage, edify, and train the members and prospects in the local community. It allows people to have a sense of belonging and support. People who attend an HBS should be trained to give not only their time in attendance and service in soul winning and inviting prospects but also their financial offerings so the need of the local HBS group is met.

HBS groups must be encouraged at all times. However, be careful that the group doesn't become a self-interest group, catering only to the needs of the few; nor should you allow it to become a clique. Every HBS group must be under the direct supervision of the pastor of the local church. A local leader appointed by the pastor and recognized by the mother church must lead it. Every HBS can serve as a reservoir of prospects or people to bring to the church services.

If the location of the HBS passes the thirty-mile radius but isn't greater than fifty miles from the main church, this group can be converted into a satellite ministry.

Key People in the HBS Group

- Preacher in charge or cell group leader
- Host home
- HBS leader or coordinator
- Secretary
- Treasurer
- Usher

Satellite Ministry

A satellite ministry (SM) is another congregation and a ministry of the local church, which allows those who live past the thirty-mile radius to remain where they are. This arrangement allows members who live within the distance to worship and serve God in their particular neighborhood. This is an ideal setting if a church doesn't have a bus ministry to pick up people for the main church. It will enable the people from within the fifty-mile radius to be a positive witness in the place where they live. This will also reduce, if not take away, the feeling of frustration among members who live far from the church since they find it too hard to involve themselves in God's service and invite their friends and loved ones to attend church services.

The SM also serves as a local outreach. There is no need to organize this into a mission work since the mother church is within the fifty-mile radius. Members are encouraged to join the mother church during Sunday school and morning worship services. Members can then meet separately during Sunday evening services, midweek services, and prayer meetings.

The church in Jerusalem followed this same pattern. Since they didn't have a big building to accommodate all the members, they had many satellite congregations within the city to minister to Christian members living in the community. The Jerusalem church had multiple pastors or leaders who oversaw satellite congregations.

SM members remain actively involved in all affairs in the main church. They can be in the main church choir. Some can teach and help in Sunday school, ushering, and other areas of Christian service. In their local area, they can be involved in soul winning and invite people around the neighborhood to attend local services on Sunday evenings, prayer meetings, and home Bible study. They give their tithes, missions giving, and other offerings to the main church. Offerings not designated as tithes and missions offerings can be used to help the local expenses, and the preacher in charge can use them for local use.

The HBS can become a satellite congregation if there are four to five new families who are saved and baptized in the local area. The leader of the SM must be a licensed preacher, have a minimum of two years of institute training, or be a current student in Bible college. His appointment is preacher in charge, and if the SM congregation is able, the leader can receive monthly financial support. Since it is a ministry, all legal matters, administrative decisions, and ministerial concerns must be brought to the attention of the main church and senior pastor.

Key People in the Satellite Ministry

- Preacher in charge or satellite leader
- Worship leader
- Secretary
- Treasurer

- Usher
- Music coordinator
- Soul-winning coordinator
- Discipleship coordinator

Outreach Ministry (OM)

An outreach ministry (OM) is the initial step toward becoming a mission congregation. It begins from a HBS group outside the fifty-mile radius of the main church. It is a congregation that has the potential of becoming an independent congregation.

For an HBS to become an OM, there must be eight to ten newly saved and baptized families coming from the local area. The outreach ministry leader is addressed as the preacher in charge. His personal qualification is the same as that of the satellite minister. As an OM, the tithes and mission offerings are all remitted to the main congregation. The OM will have the same status as the SM, including the provision of the preacher's monthly support. However, when there are ten to fifteen newly saved and baptized families from the local area, the status can be converted into a mission congregation (MC).

The minimum qualification of the OM preacher in charge remains the same as that of the SM.

Key People in the Outreach Ministry

- Preacher in charge
- Worship leader
- Secretary
- Treasurer
- Sunday school superintendent
- Sunday school teachers
- Music coordinator
- Soul-winning coordinator
- Discipleship coordinator

Mission Congregation (MC)

A mission congregation (MC) is one step before the independent congregation status. To achieve this status, the OM needs to have fifteen to twenty newly saved and baptized families from the local area. The following requirements must also be met:

The preacher in charge must be appointed and formally designated as a mission pastor and may receive monthly support. The tithes and offerings are kept in the local bank account.

Ten percent of all the tithes and offerings, not including mission giving, will need to be remitted to a clearinghouse to support new congregations and missions being established directly under the local church.

All mission offerings must be remitted to the main church through the mission board or task force to help support new congregations and world missions. The MC can designate the recipient of the mission money as long as the missionary is from a church of like faith and practice.

The MC must be financially independent and able to take care of the rental facility of the church, its promotions, and pastoral support and allowances.

Key People in a Mission Congregation

- Mission pastor
- Assistant to the mission pastor
- Finance director
- Treasurer
- Secretary or historian
- Sunday school director
- Soul-winning director
- Discipleship director
- Sunday school teachers
- Ushering director
- Facility coordinator

Independent Congregation

When the MC has twenty or more saved and baptized families locally, is financially stable, and has developed a full program for all members—such as adult, children, music, soul winning, discipleship, youth, and ushering—it can then become an independent local church upon the decision and recommendation of the senior pastor to the mother church. An assessment needs to be done, and the conditions given must be met, including the 70 percent first generational membership and the ability to support its mission pastor on a full-time basis. There must also be a mission pastor who is qualified to handle the congregation and is called and ordained by the mother church.

The local church doesn't intend to overlook the importance of the church ministerial standard. The MC must provide proof or evidence of stability to the senior pastor, who will give the recommendation to the mother church. A local pastor must then be called and installed with the recommendation from the senior pastor and jointly approved by the main church and the mission congregation. When this happens, the independent congregation (IC) will be totally independent from the main church and from the senior pastor.

The independent congregation can still consider the senior pastor as pastor emeritus, a symbolic, noncontrolling position. It can also choose to select their name that is unique to them, but the author's recommendation is to retain the name of the mother church to maintain common identity.

It is also recommended, as a sign of courtesy to the church that helped them and to the senior pastor, that the IC continues to support the church-planting ministry regularly and also support other congregations, affiliates, and missionaries connected with the mother church.

The independent congregation must bear in mind the goal of the local church, which the founder, the Lord Jesus Christ, gave, to go and plant more churches for His glory.

Key People in an Independent Church

- Pastor
- Assistant pastor
- Pastoral assistants
- Board of deacons
- Board of trustees
- Church historian
- Finance officer
- Music director
- Sunday school director
- Soul-winning director
- Discipleship director
- Facility coordinator

Chapter 8
MINISTRIES OF THE NEW TESTAMENT CHURCH

The programs in the local church must be derived from the mandate God has given. By mandate, I mean the Great Commission the Lord Jesus Christ gave and the first-century churches practiced, as recorded in the book of Acts. Although this mandate was proclaimed and commanded to the church before Jesus's ascension to heaven, it was already being practiced and fulfilled during the time of the apostles, only in a smaller scale and within a limited scope.

The general mandate was given in Matthew 28:18–20. "And Jesus came and spake unto them, saying, All power is given unto me in heaven and in earth. Go ye therefore, and teach all nations, baptizing them in the name of the Father, and of the Son, and of the Holy Ghost: Teaching them to observe all things whatsoever I have commanded you: and, lo, I am with you alway, even unto the end of the world. Amen."

This mandate is a command the Lord gave to the church to prepare disciples to do the specific works of the Lord found in Luke 4:18–19. "The Spirit of the Lord is upon me, because he hath anointed me to preach the gospel to the poor; he hath sent me to heal the brokenhearted, to preach deliverance to the captives, and recovering of sight to the blind, to set at liberty them that are bruised, To preach the acceptable year of the Lord."

Soul-Winning Ministry

This ministry is considered the priority of the church. The church must provide opportunity for all members to fulfill the task of reaching the community with the gospel of the Lord Jesus Christ, one soul at a time. The International Bible Baptist Church is so committed to this task that soul winners are regularly trained using Dr. David Wood's Operation Go.

Operation Go is a dynamic and systematic approach of gospel presentation that can be taught to everyone in the church. This program allows trainees to go through a series of thirteen lessons under the supervision of a mentor. While they are being trained, immediate application is encouraged simultaneously with each lesson. This can be done regularly once a week or every Saturday at ten o'clock during the saturation program, in which soul winners go to the community and knock on doors. This is an on-going ministry, led by the soul-winning director.

Everybody must be involved in soul winning, from the pastor down to the newest member. Aggressively promote this to the church during services through testimonies, recognition of those who have successfully won souls over the past week, and goal setting to train more soul winners.

If members are unable to join during the regular soul-winning weekly campaign, encourage them to do so during their own time. Never allow pride to set in. This usually occurs when people tend to be proud of their soul-winning achievements. Remember, it is God who saves. We are merely instruments of the gospel. Also, soul winning is just the beginning. From there the next step is to follow up on the souls saved.

Follow-Up Ministry

Following up on those who have been saved is a vital ministry to fulfill the mandate. Without this, prospects fail to grow and mature in their faith.

The goal is to get the prospect committed to the next step of his or Christian life—in other words, believer's baptism. Without this spiritual commitment, the prospect won't grow in spirituality. This approach includes visiting those who attended the previous church services and encouraging them to come back and possibly join the church. It is done through the following:

1. A letter from the pastor

   A personal letter to visitors thanks them for attending the services. This letter is sent the day after church attendance to advise prospects of regular services and other ministries available in the local church.

2. A phone call from the church staff or a member

   Through phone contact, the visitors or prospects are thanked for attending the services, and an appointment is also made for a personal visit. The phone call must be made within the week after church attendance.

3. A personal visit

   A member of the pastoral staff personally makes this visit. It is always good for a church leader to visit and answer whatever questions visitors may have about the church. This visit also allows the pastoral staff to share what assurance of salvation is and explain baptism. The personal visit must be completed during the first week after attendance and should be followed up on monthly.

The purpose of the follow-up ministry is to make disciples under the teaching of the word of God; follow-up is done through the next step of discipleship and fellowship.

Discipleship and Fellowship Ministry

This provides the opportunity to teach new converts and members the doctrines and practices of the church based on the word of God. The purpose of discipleship is not only to gain biblical knowledge but also to see the disciple duplicate himself or herself in another person. For this to work, the disciple must learn to be a "discipler" or mentor to a new disciple. The goal is to see every disciple serve the Lord faithfully and consistently until the return of Christ (1 Cor. 4:2). This can be done using different methods.

The most common method is discipleship through mentoring. This is also called the one-on-one approach and is considered the most effective method used since the time of the apostles. The Lord and the apostle Paul were both known to use this approach. This is a method every leader must engage in to mold and personally train another leader for the Lord Jesus Christ.

First John is a great book to start with a disciple. It explains that joy can be achieved through fellowshipping with other believers based on fellowship with the Father and the Son. Joy is the result of having the Spirit in our hearts. However, joy can never be realized without the idea of Christlikeness. Christlikeness can never be achieved without a mature Christian modeling it to a young disciple. It must be learned, and the discipler should intimate it to a disciple.

Fellowship is the biblical word for mentoring. It is done by showing disciples how to live the Christian life. It means modeling the life of Christ through Christian behavior and character. In human relationships, it can be called "bonding." It has been proved that bonding is important in every form of relationship. It is true with husbands and wives, parents and children, and newly born babies and the parents, especially the mother.

This is also true with spiritual children. They need a pattern or model to learn Christian behavior and character from. I have designed the Fellowship in Action Discipleship Program as a tool to help young believers know the Lord in the most intimate way. It has a threefold objective:

1. To help strengthen the disciple and maintain fellowship with the Lord Jesus Christ to conform to His image
2. To encourage believers to be living and serving disciples of the Lord Jesus Christ and make the principles of Christianity relevant in their lives and in the people around them

3. To win another person and make him or her a disciple of Jesus Christ. It is to train him or her to be a discipler for another.

The aim of discipleship ministry is to help every disciple develop spiritual discipline until the godly and biblical principles become his or her lifestyle. It is based on the five spiritual needs of man. This ministry will allow relationships to become what they should be for the glory of God.

1. Fellowship in word

This is mentoring around the word of God. It is a regular time each week a discipler has to spend with a disciple to study and memorize the word of God. The disciple or discipleship team must commit to read the Bible through in a year by selecting a passage to read daily for one's Bible study and quiet time. Compare notes based on individual study. Refer to a reputable and sound discipleship manual. The one we use at IBBC is the *Like a Tree Discipleship Manual*. Memorize a verse a week.

John 15:3, 7 says, "Now ye are clean through the word which I have spoken unto you … If ye abide in me, and my words abide in you, ye shall ask what ye will, and it shall be done unto you."

2. Fellowship in prayer

This is a prayer covenant between the mentor and the disciple. A time is spent to share and bring requests before the throne of God in prayer. It teaches the disciple how to communicate with God by means of prayer and explains that prayer is not only asking but also an act of worshipping God. The mentor and disciple must form a prayer partnership by selecting a common time to pray. They must meet once a week to share prayer requests and answered prayers using prayer lists and prayer cards.

Ephesians 6:18 says, "Praying always with all prayer and supplication in the Spirit, and watching thereunto with all perseverance and supplication for all saints."

3. Fellowship in service

This is when the mentor guides his or her disciple to serve God in the local church. This service applies what has been learned in obedience to what God has commanded. Every disciple must be encouraged to serve. The team must determine disciples' gifts, talents, and abilities; and encourage them to get involved in the service of the Lord immediately.

Try to encourage involvement by serving together in one endeavor until disciples become interested and settled to be on their own. Examples of Christian service new disciples can engage in include the bus ministry, choir, ushering, tract distribution, visitation, and so forth. Have the church come up with a list of ministries and priorities available for their personal involvement.

John 15:10, 14 says, "If ye keep my commandments, ye shall abide in my love; even as I have kept my Father's commandments, and abide in his love ... Ye are my friends, if ye do whatsoever I command you."

4. Fellowship in action

This step will show the disciple how to live and appropriately respond to daily life situations. It shows the young in the faith how to live right according to the will of God. Develop friendship not only on the spiritual level but also on the casual level, but to avoid complications, such fellowship must be between the same genders. Share some fun by doing something together, such as sports, hobbies, and so forth. Learn to know each other's desires, likes, and dislikes. Show the disciple that you are also human like he or she is and capable of committing mistakes. Show that it is normal (human) to fall but not to stand; yet because we are in Christ, we can stand.

John 15:12–15 says, "This is my commandment, That ye love one another, as I have loved you. Greater love hath no man than this, that a man lay down his life for his friends. Ye are my friends, if ye do whatsoever I command you. Henceforth I call you not servants; for the servant knoweth not what his lord doeth: but I have called you friends; for all things that I have heard of my Father I have made known unto you."

5. Fellowship in motion

This is the stage when the mentor and disciple disengage from each other to win a new disciple to work on. This completes the cycle of fellowship to start another cycle. Teach and encourage each other to win and build souls for the glory of God. Again, applying the elements of fellowship, nurture the new disciple to conform to the image of the Lord Jesus Christ (Rom. 8:29). Immediately get the new convert to become part of the local church. John 15:16 says, "Ye have not chosen me, but I have chosen you, and ordained you, that ye should go and bring forth fruit, and that your fruit should remain."

Christian Education Ministry

The last part of the mandate in Matthew 28:20 states, "Teaching them to observe all things whatsoever I have commanded you: and, lo, I am with you alway, even unto the end of the world. Amen."

Christian education is a necessity in the ministry of the church. It completes the mandate and guarantees the perpetuation and effectiveness of the plan of God. Without this, the work of the Lord cannot be sustained. This is God's design to keep the gospel moving. It must be addressed seriously and responsibly.

While preaching motivates, challenges, and exhorts church members of the church, teaching informs, educates, trains, and helps members understand the principles of God to serve with wisdom and power. This step can be done in several ways, and the most effective one is through the Sunday school or Sabbath School.

The primary purpose of Christian education is the greater edification of believers. Many churches use Sunday school primarily for numerical growth. Having a high attendance is great and must be encouraged. However, it isn't the main goal of Christian education. That is spiritual edification. Good spiritual feeding, which is greatly edifying, will result in church growth both numerically and spiritually.

Therefore, Christian education is designed to teach the saved and baptized members of the church to be complete in Christ. This needs to be emphasized since in most churches today the approach is generic Christianity. The mandate is very clear: the teaching must be introduced only after the believer obeys God in baptism. Short of this requirement is like feeding "pearls to the swine." Many people have accumulated knowledge without taking on the responsibility of serving God in the church. They have used the nuggets of God for personal gain in vain.

The knowledge of the word of God is specially given to those willing to live the word. James 1:22 aptly says, "But be ye doers of the word, and not hearers only, deceiving your own selves."

Unbelievers who attend the Sunday school hour may be given the message of salvation through evangelism or a gospel class. It is wise to place those who are saved but not baptized in a separate class such as the New Convert's Class.

Dr. David Wood's Sunday School Directors' Institute offers great material to train workers in the local church. It provides information on Christian education to allow church growth not only numerically but also spiritually.

The Pastor and the Sunday School Staff

The pastor plays an important role in the success of the Sunday school ministry. His authority and involvement will greatly encourage members to support the ministry. In doing so, he must appoint a Sunday school director or administrator to run and manage the ministry under his supervision. This person must oversee the staff, curriculum, and school's operation. The pastor's responsibilities include the following:

1. Develop a mission statement.
2. Define and clarify the role of each staff member.
3. Choose the Sunday school administrator or director.
4. Screen and appoint qualified Sunday school workers.

5. Choose a godly, age-appropriate, and relevant curriculum.
6. Regularly consult with the director, administrator, or superintendents of each department and with the staff.
7. Supervise all Sunday school promotions.
8. Regularly promote and announce the ministry publicly.
9. Organize Sunday school classes using age-appropriate materials and approaches with relevance in this generation.
10. Organize efficient record keeping.
11. Spend time in prayer with the Sunday school staff.

The Sunday school director or administrator is directly responsible to the pastor. His or her responsibilities include the following:

1. Direct the whole Sunday school operation.
2. Supervise the Sunday school superintendents.
3. Assist in the selection and appointing of teachers.
4. Help in choosing the curriculum.
5. Meet regularly with the staff.
6. Direct all Sunday school promotions.
7. Supervise record keeping.
8. Encourage superintendents.
9. Participate in soul winning.

A small church can have three Sunday school departments: children, youth, and adults. The Sunday school superintendent is the department head. His or her responsibilities include the following:

1. Be directly responsible to the Sunday school director or administrator.
2. Supervise all the teachers.
3. Meet with the teaching staff regularly.
4. Supervise record keeping.
5. Maintain the supply of teachers.
6. Visit and encourage the teachers.
7. Regularly monitor the progress of the ministry.
8. Participate in soul winning.

Sunday school teachers are the most important members of this ministry. They are the people directly engaged in teaching and supervising the students. Their responsibilities include the following:

1. Prepare the Sunday school materials prayerfully and thoroughly.
2. Be directly responsible to the Sunday school superintendent.
3. Appoint or elect the Sunday school officers.
4. Organize the class officers.
5. Supervise the class record keeping.
6. Visit and encourage each member regularly.
7. Visit the absentees in their homes.
8. Be sensitive to the spiritual needs and concerns of each member.
9. Participate in soul winning.

Sunday School Class Divisions

The Sunday school lessons can be imparted more effectively to students who are grouped together appropriately. In such cases, the commonality between the members of the class enables the teacher to give relevant examples and the students to ask questions regarding less general issues. This sort of interaction facilitates better learning. The following are some suggested class divisions for members to reap maximum benefits from Sunday school:

Class Divisions by Age Appropriateness

Simple Division
This is best for a new church or small congregation setup.

Nursery: birth to two years
Beginner: preschool to kindergarten five
Primary: grades one to three
Intermediate: grades four to six
Youth: grades seven to twelve
Adults: college and up

Expandable Division 1
This is best for a church of sixty to two hundred members.

Nursery: birth to two years
Beginner: preschool to kindergarten
Primary boys: grades one to three
Primary girls: grades one to three
Intermediate boys: grades four to six
Intermediate girls: grades four to six
Junior high: grades seven to eight
Youth: grades nine to twelve
College and career: college students and unmarried professionals
Adults: married adults and other seniors

Expandable Division 2
This is best for a church of two hundred to three hundred members.

Nursery (birth to two years)
    Crib: birth to twelve months
    Toddler: twelve months to two years
Preschool: ages three to four
Beginner: ages five to six

Primary (grades one to three)
    Boys 1: grades one to two
    Boys 2: grade three
    Girls 1: grades one to two
    Girls 2: grade three

Intermediate (grades four to six)
    Boys 1: grades four to five
    Boys 2: grade six
    Girls 1: grades four to five
    Girls 2: grade six

Youth (grades seven to twelve)
    Junior high boys: grades seven to eight
    Junior high girls: grades seven to eight
    Senior high: grades nine to twelve

Adults (high school graduates and up)
College and career: single high school graduates and college students
Young married class: married high school graduates and college students
Regular adults: other adults under sixty years old
Senior adults: sixty years and older

Class Divisions by Relevance

Class divisions among children must be based on age appropriateness and their behavior upon entry to the Sunday school class. Among the youth and adults, it's best to consider their specific needs and divide classes based on relevance. Some examples of such classes are the following:

Gospel Class: this is designed for unsaved visitors and those unsure of their salvation.

Visitors' Class: this is designed for first-time attendees looking for a church. The purpose of the class is to orient visitors about the various ministries and opportunities for service.

New Converts' Class: this is designed for the newly saved and baptized in the church.

Doctrine Class: this is designed for those seeking to learn more from the word of God.

Spiritual Life Class: this is a class with a practical Christianity approach. It is the next class after the New Converts' Class.

Youth for the World Class: this is designed to teach the youth how to conduct themselves in this modern world.

Seniors' Class: this is designed for senior citizens.

Pastors' Class: this is designed for preachers and leaders of the church.

Marriage Encounter Class: this is a special class designed to help and strengthen marital relationships.

Parenting Class: this is a special class designed to teach parents biblical parenting principles.

Financial Stewardship Class: this is a special class designed for those facing financial concerns.

Christian Liberty Class: this is a special class designed for those in bondage due to addictions (drugs, alcohol, gambling, and so forth).

Promotions and Campaigns

To maintain interest and sustain the progress in the local church ministry, Sunday school promotions are encouraged. This will increase awareness of the importance of Sunday school and allow members to actively participate. Moreover, it will increase the attendance and bond of fellowship and excitement among students. Some popular promotions are the following:

1. Each One Bring One Campaign
2. Baccalaureate Sunday
3. Mother's Day
4. Father's Day
5. Patriotic Sunday
6. Neighbor's Sunday
7. Friend's Sunday

8. Back-to-School Sunday
9. Thanksgiving Sunday
10. Stewardship Sunday
11. Christmas Sunday

These campaigns must be planned, organized, and carried out through the whole year. Promote each campaign with excitement and allow every member to participate by inviting visitors to come. Tokens may be given away. An appropriate lesson will highlight the occasion.

The Sunday school ministry can boost the attendance of the church through promotions and campaigns. The purpose of these campaigns is not only to swell the attendance but also to gather more people to listen to the gospel of salvation. The preparation must be focused on spiritual reproduction.

Attendance Growth

According to David Wood's *Sunday School Director's Institute Manual*, the law of Sunday school states that the teacher-student ratio is one is to ten. Therefore, to double your attendance, you must double your Sunday school workers. To do this, a church must function like a well-oiled machine.

Dr. Wood, considered an expert in soul winning and church planting, started two big churches before he went into full-time evangelism. He now operates a soul-winning ministry that has helped many churches and pastors worldwide. He believes that for a church to grow, it must have the following features, like those of a working copier machine:

1. The Feeder (outreach): a ministry to reach the people so they will come to church, such as soul winning, saturation, and so forth
2. The Image (public service): the image people see. The impression attracts people to come and remain. This includes the facility, music ministry, nursery, media, bulletin, and so forth.

3. The Keeper (discipleship): a program that will make church members regularly come and be loyal to the church, such as Sunday school, mentoring, and so forth

These three operations must be ongoing to maintain growth and balance in the ministry. To follow the Sunday school law, a church with an attendance of one hundred can double if twenty people are trained to work. This is an attainable goal. There is no reason for a church not to grow.

First, the outreach ministry must get people saved and baptized on a regular basis. Among those reached with the gospel, there are some who will volunteer to serve in Sunday school and other ministries.

Second, to motivate people and encourage faithfulness in the service of the Lord, the church's public image must be excellent. This includes cleanliness of facilities, auditoriums, classrooms, and restrooms. Brochures and bulletins must be presentable. The choir and music must be organized.

Third, a Christ-centered Sunday school will help people turn to Christ for encouragement and faithfulness, though keeping people in church is the hardest task to do. Churches tend to please people rather than God. To bring balance, an effective Sunday school program must be in place, solely focused on the person of Christ, the only effective attraction and the ultimate motivation for people to stay.

Fishers of Men

By Hernes M. Abante
October 6, 1998

We have come here today
To declare our trust in God, come what may.
Let us go, let's declare,
Let us shout the gospel message all the way.

Jesus Christ, He commands
We should not allow our fears to defeat His plan.
On we go; follow Him.
Let's be brave to launch as fishers of men.

We are here for You, Lord,
All prepared to go and carry the word
To all nations on earth,
For we want all to know Your saving grace.

We'll lift Your name to the world.
With Your pow'r we'll raise your banner unfurled.
On we go; heed the call
As members of the soul-winner's fold.

Chapter 9
SERVICE OPPORTUNITIES

The mandate must come full circle. The church should help believers get baptized, be taught, and have an opportunity to serve the Lord with their God-given abilities. The goal is to bring every believer approved unto God.

On average, only 20 percent of church members are involved in church ministry. The remaining 80 percent are mere spectators, either doing something minimally or nothing at all. This is also true in the area of stewardship of giving—a sad commentary of most churches today.

Believers in the service of the Lord are growing and glowing servants of Christ. They have joy and peace in their hearts, knowing they are doing God's will in their lives. Because they are busy serving and pleasing the Lord, these faithful servants have no time to scrutinize and criticize the works of others. While they do their business well and responsibly, they continue to encourage others to do the same. Their faithfulness commands respect and serves as an excellent example for others to emulate.

Idleness invites sin in the heart. When people are idle and not serving the Lord, they have more time to criticize others. They are discontented and unhappy in their Christian lives. They complain more than they help. They are stagnant in their faith and miserable in their attitude. They are people who like to see other people get down to their level of misery by their negative pattern of behavior. They are like cancer cells that will eventually affect every member in the body to his or her destruction.

The Church Must be Dynamic

The church must be active, full of life and opportunities for all members to serve. Every ministry in the church is a place of service. It is important, however, for a church to assess the calling and attitude of each member. When assigning a task to a member, the will of God, not the will of man, must be followed. Let us consider 1 Corinthians 1:24–29.

> But unto them who are called, both Jews and Greeks, Christ the power of God, and the wisdom of God. Because the foolishness of God is wiser than men; and the weakness of God is stronger than men. For you see your calling, brethren, how that not many wise men after the flesh, not many mighty, not many noble, are called: But God has chosen the foolish things of the world to confound the wise; and God has chosen the weak things of the world to confound the things which are mighty; And base things of the world, and things which are despised, has God chosen, yea, and things which are not, to bring to nothing things that are: That no flesh should glory in his presence.

In the service of the Lord, we need the power and wisdom of God, because man's wisdom and abilities will never qualify man for Christian service. God doesn't need experts in the ministries. He needs obedient and dedicated servants who are willing to be trained and are always available to do the job according to His will. The greatest ability is availability to be used of God.

This truth is vital because many people serve in the church based on their abilities and expertise, which give way to pride and arrogance. In my years in the service of the Lord, I have seen this behavior ruin people's lives and the ministry countless times. I can recall one incident when I was the music director of a church. A young lady approached me and bragged that, since she was trained in voice and had received so many awards in her singing career, I needed to assign her to sing in the choir. She added that her voice would provide the help the choir needed so badly in the soprano part. I quickly reminded her that her singing voice was a gift from God, but since it was infected by the spirit of pride, she first needed to surrender her voice to the Lord before it could be used for His glory. She immediately got the message.

We Are Recruits, Not Volunteers!

It is tempting for a pastor or ministry leader to compromise to get able people to serve. Who wouldn't want to have qualified and talented people in the church? Should we ignore and put to naught their abilities? How do we keep the standard and retain talented and qualified people?

This is the dilemma we all face in getting volunteers for the service of the Lord. I used the word *volunteer* because that is how people often consider themselves to justify their non-commitment to the ministry. "I only volunteered, and I am not being paid; therefore …" "I don't need to agree with your standards. I volunteer because you need me."

These are statements I hear many people say in regard to their attitude to the work of the Lord. It is sad that we have so many experts and "prima donnas" in most churches today. The attraction is no longer God.

To avoid this problem, the pastor of the church must make it totally clear that God's work isn't a volunteer work. It is our service to our Master and Lord. It is an act of obedience and submission from a faithful servant. To serve God is a great privilege. We work because we need to serve God and obey His will. We serve in the church to glorify and worship Him with all the abilities and wisdom He has given to us. Having a firm understanding of the proper motivation of service for the Lord will keep us from being proud, arrogant, and self-righteous.

Guidelines for Christian Service

Every member needs to be prepared for service, and opportunities must be available to fit the readiness of each individual in the local church. The guidelines are the following:

1. Explain to members the real motivation for service before assessing their abilities and the areas where they fit.
2. Encourage members to surrender their knowledge, wisdom, and abilities to God.
3. Allow members to first submit to a mentor and learn their position in the ministry based on Christian character and humility.

You may have noticed that these guidelines are more focused on right behavior and not on abilities, because we know abilities come from God, who is able to bless us with different gifts and talents to accomplish His perfect will in our lives.

It is a standing rule that only members of the church can serve. However, to motivate people who are still ambivalent about membership, it is often wise to allow some the taste of Christian service on a case-to-case basis. Some people must have the "feel" first before they will commit. This tendency is part of human nature. It is also important that when they are allowed to try, it will be only for a limited period. They need to make a decision soon or within a certain time. To protect the interest, purity, and testimony of the church, only those people who come from churches of like faith and practice must be given this opportunity.

Service Opportunities

Opportunities for service are abundant in a growing and dynamic church. Progress doesn't stop and is never stagnant. There are always activities and opportunities available at all times.

Service Opportunities for New Members

1. Singing in the choir
2. Soul winning
3. Ushering
4. Assisting in Sunday school
5. Assisting in junior church
6. Helping with building maintenance

Service Opportunities for Faithful Members

1. Choir and special numbers
2. Worship team (music)
3. Visitation and soul winning
4. Teaching positions in the Sunday school
5. Elected positions (administration)
6. Facility upkeep and supervision
7. Nursery
8. Junior church

Service Opportunities for Members with Leadership Qualities

1. Elected positions (administration)
2. Appointed position of leadership assigned by the pastor
3. Chairmanship
4. Administrative and ministrative leadership position
5. Layperson leadership
6. Board of trustees

Service Opportunities for People with a Special Calling from the Lord

1. Ministry of preaching
2. Ministry of teaching
3. Ministry of exhortation or counseling
4. Board of deacons
5. Pastoral assistant
6. Assistant pastor
7. Mission pastor
8. Preacher in charge
9. Director of ministries

Church Ministries in Need of Staff Support

1. Music ministry: director, choir, vocal, instrumental, and worship team
2. Media ministry
3. Worship: worship leader
4. Ushering: welcoming and offering
5. Sunday school: director, superintendents, teachers
6. Junior church: preacher in charge
7. Patch the Pirate[2]: director and assistants
8. Soul winners and visitation workers
9. Ladies' fellowship
10. Men's fellowship
11. House of Martha[3]
12. Academy: principal and teaching staff
13. ACTS preachers

---

[2] The Patch the Pirate is a children's discipleship program that is done weekly in a Church using Bible verses, songs, and series of Bible lessons. It is normally done during Sunday evening or Mid- week activity for children.

[3] The House of Martha is a fellowship of single or married ladies who are focused on serving in the local Church

14. Youth ministry: director and youth workers
15. Children's ministry: director and workers
16. Facility maintenance
17. Prayer warriors
18. Office workers
19. Youth for the world
20. Mission task force
21. School task force
22. Institute: teachers
23. Home Bible study leaders
24. Outreach workers

Chapter 10
CHURCH WORSHIP

The church is a place of worship. All activities, programs, and ministries in the church are there for the sole purpose of worshipping God. This is the true character and spirit of a New Testament church. In this act of worship, the only audience worthy of all our attention and praises is God.

The goal of the church isn't to please man. Even though the Lord instructed us to serve one another and minister to people, the underlying reason is still for the glory of God. The following passages clearly state this truth:

> And whatsoever ye do in word or deed, do all in the name of the Lord Jesus, giving thanks to God and the Father by him. (Col. 3:17)

> And whatsoever ye do, do it heartily, as to the Lord, and not unto men. (Col. 3:23)

The instructions in the above passages also include everything we do outside the church. In this life, the focus is to please, serve, and worship God. There are three major areas of worship in the church: worship in word, worship in music, and worship in the stewardship of giving.

Worship in Word

The pastor leads worship in word when he summons believers to hear the word of the Lord. The purpose is to listen to God's instructions as He speaks through His servant. During this time, the pastor or preacher is the voice of the Lord, and the people's responsibility is to listen with an attentive heart. Listening to the message is giving all the attention to our awesome God as He speaks through His servant and letting the Holy Spirit convict the heart to respond.

God ministers to us as we listen to His "still small voice" (1 Kings 19:12). Yes, we hear the audible and sometimes loud voice of the preacher, but behind that voice is the tender and compassionate voice of the Lord as He rebukes, encourages, instructs, and reproves us with "all longsuffering and doctrine." Second Timothy 4:2 says, "Preach the word; be instant in season, out of season; reprove, rebuke, exhort with all longsuffering and doctrine."

Intently listening and giving God our full attention to what He says is an act of sincere worship. It is recognizing His authority and will over us. The attitude of submission to His word is well pleasing unto the Lord.

Since the ministry of preaching is given to the pastors of the church, it is therefore essential for him to always be prepared. The scriptures make it clear that the preacher must "preach the Word; be instant in season, out season" (2 Timothy 4:2).

Preaching is a lifetime preparation and a special calling from God. Since it is a special calling, a preacher must face his responsibility seriously through a surrendered life evident in his diligent study of the word of God. In Second Timothy 2:15, the apostle Paul instructed his Bible student, Timothy, to study as he was preparing for the ministry. "Study to shew thyself approved unto God, a workman that needeth not to be ashamed, rightly dividing the word of truth."

Let us consider several truths from this passage:

1. "Study" means having the discipline to spend time learning the word of God with diligence.

2. "Show ourselves" means we need to show that we are able servants before men and God. It also means that the primary responsibility of every believer is to learn from the word of God.

3. "Approved unto God": We please nobody but God. The ultimate judge of our motives and action is God. We work to be approved of God.

4. "A workman": A preacher is a workman who is skillful in what he does. It takes discipline to learn and be effective.

5. "Needeth not to be ashamed": Testimony is at stake here. Prepare well to preach right.

6. "Rightly dividing the Word of Truth": Follow a systematic approach in studying the word. Bring out the proper interpretation of the word and apply it correctly.

7. To be skilled and effective in preaching the word, the preacher must develop through training is skills in two areas of discipline. These are homiletics and hermeneutics, which are both considered an art and branch of study.

8. Homiletics is the art of preaching.

9. Homiletics refers to the physical and verbal presentation of the message. It is how you project yourself as a preacher to the audience or the listeners. It includes the following:

   1. Appropriate physical appearance
   2. Vocal projection
   3. Style of delivery or communication approach
   4. Proper use of language, illustrations, and other tools of communication
   5. Pulpit mannerisms
   6. Pulpit presence, including eye contact
   7. Organized sermon outline

According to James Braga in his book *How to Prepare Bible Messages*, a sermon isn't an essay or literary composition intended to be read and reread. It's a message intended to be heard and to have an immediate impact on listeners.

He further states that to make this impact, a sermon must be free from ambiguity and contain no material extraneous to its main theme. It must have a distinct form or pattern, its ideas must indicate continuity of thought, and it must move toward a goal or climax.

A preacher must be a skillful artisan to effectively convey the message of Christ into the hearts of the people. He is an artist and a scientist the Holy Spirit controls to express the will of God in a clear voice. To do this, he must be skillful not only in the art and science of interpretation but also in homiletics.

It is therefore necessary for a preacher to know his craft well. The way he stands before the pulpit and expresses himself in words is a testimony not only of God's grace but also of his total surrender to the task he has been assigned to do. Consider the areas where a preacher needs to be effective:

Appropriate Physical Appearance

How you appear before the people already presents a message. Be appropriate by wearing the best attire available to represent the Lord. In choosing your attire, you need to be sensitive to the culture. It's best to wear something your audience can relate to. For example, you wouldn't want to wear a tuxedo or a three-piece suit in a third-world country or a barong tagalog during a winter in Utah.

Vocal Projection

Vocal command must be strong to be effective in oral communication. Strength doesn't necessarily mean loud and threatening. A preacher needs to know how to modulate his voice for proper emphasis. You can be loud, soft, whispery, and animated. All these can enhance your vocal delivery. It's important for a preacher to know how to use his diaphragm so as not to ruin his voice. A preacher must learn to shout in whisper and to scream in silence.

Style of Delivery or Communication Approach

Preachers are public speakers and as such must know varied styles and approaches of delivery or elocution. People tend to respond effectively to a particular style of preaching. Styles can be modified or enhanced by using multimedia, animation, humor, or statistics; or they can be changed from a teaching style to a formal preaching style. Avoid being monotonous in your delivery. Communication isn't effective or doesn't take place if the preacher isn't understood or the message doesn't come across to listeners. Keep in mind that communication is a two-way process.

Proper Use of Language, Illustrations, and Other Tools of Communication

It is imperative for a preacher to use all the necessary tools to allow effective communication. This includes the use of language the people are accustomed to hearing and understanding. It further includes body language. This advice is useful if the church is located in a multiethnic community. When using illustrations or other tools of communication, be culturally sensitive to avoid any provocations that can trigger negative reactions from the listeners. This is especially true if you want to use humor in your delivery.

Avoiding Pulpit Mannerisms and Speech Impediments

Mannerisms are the body's defense mechanism when someone is subjected to stress. They come out unconsciously and can become a hindrance to the effective transmission of the message. Avoid annoying mannerisms in the pulpit. To minimize this problem, practice in front of a mirror, identify the mannerisms, and practice some more to eliminate these. Some mannerisms I have noticed are scratching and picking the nose, zipping and unzipping the fly of the pants, buttoning and unbuttoning the shirt, scratching the head, and a lot more. Speech impediments to be avoided are stuttering, stammering, mental block, and so forth.

Pulpit Presence, Including Eye Contact

Audience contact is important for communication to be effective. It refers to the way you project your confidence to people with your presence in the pulpit. As a servant of God, one needs to show boldness and confidence in the work of the Lord. A preacher needs to project an image that he knows exactly what he is talking about. Confidence is communicated by looking directly into the eyes of the listeners to show that the preacher is sincere and means well.

Organized Sermon Outline

This tool directly benefits the preacher. It organizes his thoughts and allows the delivery to be smooth, direct, and spontaneous. Outlining provides the structure of the message. It serves as a guide but allows imagination and creativity to run its course. More importantly, it allows the Holy Spirit to take control of the preacher's mind.

A manuscript enslaves the preacher. Since all details and words are written down, the manuscript doesn't enable you to project confidence, because your eyes are focused only on reading what you have to say. This result doesn't allow spontaneity and creativity. The Holy Spirit doesn't have control.

A proper sermon outline or homiletic structure is an invaluable tool to a preacher. Learn to create an outline and use it properly. Here's an outline I use for my own sermon preparation:

Title:
Date/Occasion:
Text:

Introduction:
    1.
    2.

Transitional Statement:

I.   First Major Point
     A.   First Subpoint
     B.   Second Subpoint

II. Second Major Point
     A.   First Subpoint
     B.   Second Subpoint

III. Third Major Point
     A.   First Subpoint
     B.   Second Subpoint

Conclusion:
     1.
     2.

An outline must be brief. It serves as a useful aid to a preacher because it enables him to see the entire message at a glance. Let me explain each part of the outline:

The Title

Usually one of the last parts to be prepared, the title serves a significant role because it is what the listener remembers the most. It carries the subject or theme of the message. It is the message in a capsule expressed in one simple word or statement.

1. The title must relate with the whole message or text.
2. It must be simple, catchy, and interesting.
3. It must be brief but not abrupt. We must not sacrifice clarity for the sake of brevity.
4. It can be stated in different forms of statement; namely, declarative, interrogative, and exclamatory.

5. It must relate to the body of the message or the major points.
6. It must be connected to the conclusion.

The Date or Occasion

It is wise to include the date or message occasion to help a busy preacher schedule its delivery to avoid embarrassing repetitions.

The Text

A Bible message must always be supported by a scripture text, be it a major text, a supporting text, or a springboard text. It must be primarily based on the word of God, not on current events or news of the day.

The Introduction

This is a statement that attracts, captures, or hooks the audience to listen. It also prepares the minds of listeners and secures their interest to listen attentively.

1. The introduction must be clear, brief, and interesting.
2. It should lead to the main idea of the message.
3. It must be relevant to get the attention of listeners.

The Transitional Statement

It is a statement that expresses in a complete sentence the main idea of the message. It is also called the "proposition," and it carries the exegetical idea or expository unit of the main text or the message as a whole.

1. The transitional statement must express the main idea of the message in a complete sentence.
2. It must be a declarative sentence.

3. It must be a timeless truth expressed in the present tense.
4. It must be stated clearly and with simplicity.
5. It must be specific.
6. It should be stated briefly and with clarity.
7. It must be related to or lead to the main points of the message.

The Major Points or Divisions of the Message

The main body of the message is arranged systematically and progressively to promote clarity of thought and assist the preacher in the proper treatment of the subject.

1. The main points or divisions must grow out of the transitional statement.
2. Each must be independent of, but complementary to, each other.
3. The main points must progress logically, where each main division contributes to the development of the message.
4. The main points must be supported by collateral or supporting verses, illustrations, and other tools to make the message progressively clear.
5. Each main point must convey a single idea bridged with transitional statements.
6. Its expressions must be uniform and parallel with each division.
7. As a rule, there shouldn't be more than three or four subpoints under the major points or divisions.

The Conclusion

This is the climax of the entire message, in which the preacher's aim reaches its goal in a forceful and meaningful expression. Since it is considered the most potent part of the message, it should be treated with extra care. Poorly executed, it can weaken or render the message ineffective to the listeners. A good conclusion can also make up for deficiencies in some parts of the sermons. A conclusion can be expressed in different forms: a recapitulation, a powerful illustration, an application or appeal, and a motivation or an exhortation.

1. The conclusion must be brief. It shouldn't appear as an extension of the message, thus prolonging the message.
2. It must serve to "shoot many birds at the same time," addressing the needs of believers, unbelievers, and those in need of comfort and encouragement.
3. The words or expressions used must be selected carefully and thoughtfully, since the intent of the conclusion is to challenge the heart to respond.

When properly executed, a message outline helps the preacher deliver his sermon in an organized, concise, and clear manner, capping his message with an overwhelming effect to the listeners. It gives him freedom to depend totally on the Holy Spirit, but this is not so with the manuscript, an all-written-out message format.

Kinds of Messages or Sermons

There are different kinds of messages a preacher can use. These will give pastors and preachers a variety of ways to communicate the truth effectively. However, in this study, we will consider only the three most popular and most used forms. They are topical, textual, and expository messages

Topical Message

A topical message is a message initially derived from a topic, theme, or subject. Since it is a Bible message, one cannot define it as independent from the text. It is still totally dependent on, and supported by, biblical text. It is not, however, dependent on one single text.

It is a message that begins with a theme. The main points and body of the message consist of ideas that come from the theme. The text or texts considered are used to support or justify the theme. To prepare a topical message, you need to do the following:

1. Choose the topic.
2. Choose the central idea from the topic.
3. Choose the main text or texts that support the central idea.
4. Organize the main points derived from the central idea.
5. Arrange the main points following a logical or chronological progression.
6. Select supporting texts for the main points.
7. Provide illustrations that support the major points, treating them as subpoints.
8. Provide the title, introduction, transitional statement, and conclusion.

The topical message can be used in different ways. It is used to prepare doctrinal messages or a series of messages based on relevant and pressing issues. Among its practical uses is providing messages during holidays, such as Mother's Day, Father's Day, Thanksgiving, Easter, and Christmas celebrations.

Textual Message

A textual message is different from the topical message in its approach. While a topical message begins with a theme, a textual message begins with a text. It is an approach in which the main points or divisions are derived from a brief text. The body of the message is all taken and completely dependent on the text. To prepare a textual message, you need to do the following:

1. Choose the text.
2. Choose the central idea from the text.
3. Seriously consider the context of the text.
4. Supply the main points or divisions derived from the text.

5. Arrange the main points following a logical progression.
6. Select the supporting verses linking to the main text.
7. Provide illustrations and supporting verses that serve as subpoints.
8. Provide the title, introduction, transitional statement, and conclusion.

A textual message is based on one or more passages of scripture. It is also called a "micro-expository message," because it expounds biblical truths from a brief text.

Expository Message

An expository message is considered the best approach in message preparation. It involves interpreting a "more or less extended portion of Scriptures."[4] It may consist of a few verses, an entire chapter, or even more. It is also the most extensive, time-consuming, and thought-provoking approach, but it's one that can really edify believers and allow a better understanding of the word of God.

The main points of the expository message are directly drawn from the passage. The outline consists of progressive ideas centered on that main idea, which is called the expository unit, taken from the whole text. As a rule, the minimum number to consider is four verses.

By expounding a passage of scripture properly, a pastor can provide the proper interpretation of the word of God. Interpretation refers to the message the Lord wants to convey, not to what the preacher thinks the passage means. To prepare an expository message, you need to do the following:

1. Select a "more or less extended portion of Scripture."[5]
2. Study the selected scripture passages thoroughly and carefully.
3. Select the expository unit, the dominant truth found in the passage.

[4] "A Manual on Homiletics for Bible Students," James Braga
[5] Ibid

4. Identify the characters in the passage and study the historical and cultural background of the passage for greater understanding.

5. Supply the main points derived from the passage. Significant words or phrases in the text can be used as the main points of the outline.

6. Provide the supporting verses taken from the passages. Collateral passages can be included to supply more scriptural support.

7. Organize the main points and sub points by selecting the details of the passage. Details must be treated properly but not exhaustively.

8. Make the truths relevant and practical for today.

9. Provide the title, introduction, transitional statement, and conclusion.

An expository message should be properly treated so as not to avoid giving a "running commentary" of the passage. It must be organized into a simple, coherent, and relevant message with logical progression.

Hermeneutics: The Art of Biblical Interpretation

Preparing a good message depends on correct interpretation of the word of God. It is therefore necessary for the man of God to have knowledge and understanding of the word of God. To have this understanding, a preacher needs to know the basic rules of interpretation.

The art and science of biblical interpretation is called "hermeneutics." Its purpose is to ascertain what God has said and to determine the actual and true meaning of His word. For proper interpretation, it's important for people to have the Holy Spirit in their lives. That means they must be born again and right with God. The Spirit guides man into all truth (John 14:26). He is the One who provides illumination and understanding of the mysteries of the word of God. Without Him, not even someone with much intelligence can understand the scriptures.

To understand the Bible, one must assume that the word of God is divinely inspired and the only basis of truth and practice. It is plenary and verbally inspired, which means that every word has its precise meaning, and every word has to be taken at its face value. This is the literal approach based on the use of language and expressions known during the time the passages were written. As stated in 2 Peter 1:20–21, "We have also a more sure word of prophecy; whereunto ye do well that ye take heed, as unto a light that shineth in a dark place, until the day dawn, and the day star arise in your hearts: Knowing this first, that no prophecy of the scripture is of any private interpretation."

In the study of the word of God, we should be careful not to assign any meaning to it. Our responsibility is to discover its actual meaning by studying the word systematically or by "rightly dividing the Word of Truth" (2 Tim. 2:15). This is done by interpreting the scriptures using other scriptures, as Paul said in 1 Corinthians 2:13. "Which things also we speak, not in the words which man's wisdom teacheth, but which the Holy Ghost teacheth; comparing spiritual things with spiritual."

The basic rule is to interpret the scriptures literally. That means if the word of God makes sense, don't add any other sense. Where it doesn't make sense, another passage of the scriptures can clarify it.

Another way to interpret the scriptures properly is to consider the historical and cultural background of the passage. There is nothing wrong with going back to the languages used when the word of God was originally written.

The bottom line is found in Romans 10:17. "So then faith cometh by hearing, and hearing by the word of God.

Faith gives understanding. The more we read the word, the better we will understand the word. That is how powerful and supernatural the word of God is.

The Bible, the Preserved Word of God

The Bible is the book of books. God wrote it through His chosen men to reveal Himself and His will to us. The International Bible Baptist Church believes in its plenary and verbal inspiration. *Plenary* means it is complete and absolute in its authority. *Verbal* means the Holy Ghost equally inspired every word used in the scriptures.

IBBC also believes in its eternal preservation. God declared that His words would never pass away. Matthew 24:35 says, "Heaven and earth shall pass away, but my words shall never pass away."

We affirm that the Bible we have today is the inspired word of God through divine preservation. The inspiration of the scriptures occurred with the original texts. Inspiration has not occurred again since the Bible's original writing, and it will never happen again. God, however, in His choosing and guidance through supernatural means no one understands, preserves His Word for the present and the future generation ... and forever. To explain the doctrine of preservation, there are five logical arguments to consider. These are the following:

1. Argument of the most common language: Throughout the past centuries, God has expressed Himself and preserved His word using the most common language known to man. In the Old Testament, He used the Hebrew and Aramaic languages and the "Koine" Greek in the New Testament; and in this generation, He used the English language. Through these languages, the Bible was translated, thus preserving its authority and credibility.

2. Argument of the true source: The source is important to consider if something is to be preserved. If the source is false, then the result will be faulty. The King James Bible was the only scriptures based on the textus receptus, a credible source. All other versions were derived from the faulty Wescott and Hort.

3. Argument of the tested text: The true preserved scriptures throughout the centuries underwent severe tests and persecution. The Bible continues to be the focus of ridicule and the target of annihilation to take away the true witness, which is the preserved text.

4. Argument of endurance: This argument refers to the enduring quality of the word of God. It carries with it the promises of

the Lord that His word is preserved and will endure forever. It endures because it is the true word, and the true word endures.

5. Argument of the total dependence on the power of the Holy Spirit: Other versions depend on the reader's ability to understand. No wonder they keep revising and modifying the scriptures to be understood by men. The true word of God depends not on human understanding but on the power of the Holy Spirit. What scripture would allow you to depend more on the Holy Spirit than on the preserved word of God? The word of God cannot be understood by the ability and wisdom of man. It is God who gives discernment for understanding. If an ordinary man easily understands the word of God, then the Holy Spirit has no more work to do.

It is the conviction of the International Bible Baptist Church that the preserved word of God is still with us today in the form of the King James Bible. We use it as our main text in all our readings. While we don't discourage others to use other versions to help them understand the scriptures better, we encourage all members of our local church to have the King James Bible in their possession.

Worship in Music

Music has a very special place in the local church. Music not only allows believers the opportunity to worship the Lord but also sets the mood for all members to worship God with the proper attitude. Without music, worship is incomplete. There can never be proper worship without godly music.

Music was widely used in the Old Testament. It was a fixture in temple worship so much that the whole book of Psalms was used to provide songs not only in the temple but also during the early church. To enhance the sound, musical instruments such as the harp, timbrels, wind instrument, and percussion were used to call the people to worship God.

Because of the important role music plays in worship, the devil also uses it to drive people away from the truth. It has become his most effective tool to influence the minds of people, including believers, far from the principles of God. While we have seen throughout the history how many people were brought to worship God through music, we have also seen in the last forty years how our young people have changed their behavior toward God through its demonic and negative influence.

It is distressing to know that even Christians today have joined the world in using worldly music in their churches. We now have Christian rock, gospel rap, and Christian metal rock being performed in churches and music halls today, all in the name of Christianity.

Many churches have started contemporary services to accommodate the new trend in music. Preaching time has been reduced to mere Christian exhortation and devotion to give more time to praise and worship. The standard of worship has gone down the drain. It is no longer intended to please God but rather to please man. Music and sermons have been modified to please and attract a great crowd. Churches have turned into entertainment centers and places of social gathering. Church people have become more takers than givers.

Furthermore, churches have become retail outlets, theaters, centers, and game parlors all catering to the carnal desires of the flesh ... in the name of the gospel. People are now selective: they have become choosy with the many options and different kinds of worship styles before them. How then should we approach this corrupt movement? Should we remain true to our conservative and fundamental values?

What Is Christian Music?

The church is a place of worship. When we come to church, we have only God to please. That means whatever we do must be intended to glorify and honor God. This includes music. Why then do we choose music that pleases only people? If we come to worship God, then all the music we select must be God glorifying and honoring. To understand

and know what God-glorifying music is, let us study the elements that can turn a sound into a musical tone.

Music consists of organized sounds or tones, having the elements that make them musical. Without these elements, a sound can remain just a mere sound or noise. The five elements of music are the following:

1. Melody: This refers to the tune that gives sound its direction and beauty. It is made of a succession of sounds or tones in different intervals, called the melodic line. It gives the sound its musical identity and flow. One can know music by its melody. It has the power to move emotions and communicate feelings. It is the language of the soul. It caters to the spirit. Melody can stand alone.

2. Harmony: This refers to the combination of two or more tones or melodies sung or played at the same time. It gives richness to the sound. It speaks or caters to the heart.

3. Lyrics: This refers to the words in music. It gives music the sense of reason. It caters or speaks to the mind. Like melody, the lyrics can also stand alone.

4. Timbre. This refers to the quality of the tone. It provides the sound quality or qualitative value to music. It caters to the soul.

5. Rhythm: This refers to the timing. Its job is to keep the beat in music. It caters to the flesh. It is the lowest form among the elements of music. Notice that when a beat or succession of beats is heard, the human body immediately reacts and moves.

For tones to be musical, the dominant element must be melody. The rest serves as support to enhance the melody. Christian music must be melodic to move the spirit more than the body. Christian music must be more melodic and soothing to the heart and spirit rather than have a dominant rhythm that is loud, annoying, and hard to the ears, disrupting meditation and worship.

I love orchestral music. In an orchestra rhythmic instruments, such as the drums, are situated at the back. They never create the dominant sound. The instruments in front, such as the violin and other string instruments, are all melodic instruments. To see drums occupying the center of attention in praise and worship today is bothersome.

Lyrics are also an important element, for they convey a message that influences listeners. However, a good melody can still be used to cater to the flesh with lyrics that aren't glorifying to the Lord.

Singing, like praying, is an act of worship. Some songs churches use in today's praise and worship are repetitive, like chants and mantras used in Eastern religion. Remember, the Lord Jesus Christ said, "But when ye pray, use not vain repetitions as the heathen do: for they think that they shall be heard for their much speaking" (Matt. 6:7).

We need to be extra careful not to follow the ways of the heathen to influence our worship. Our God deserves better treatment from His children. We ought not to use the vehicle of the world to convey His message to the world.

Basis of New Testament Music

Music has a very special place in my heart. I was exposed to music from a young and tender age as a soloist in the church, a member of the junior choir, a church organist at twelve years old, a pianist at sixteen, and then a music director at twenty. Here's special thanks to my mother, who gave me motivation and taught me the discipline to practice the piano for at least two hours every day. She wasn't a musical person and couldn't play any musical instruments, but her appreciation for music was commendable. I appreciate the genes from my father, who could play musical instruments and sing without any formal musical training.

After graduating from a Bible college, I underwent formal training in piano and voice in the a conservatory of music in the Philippines. As a music scholar in both disciplines, I have performed as a soloist, accompanist, and singer in my native country and in the United States. Music gave me the opportunity to support my early seminary training. While attending a seminary in San Francisco, I was a music director in several churches in Northern California. I continued to serve in that capacity for eight years until I started the International Bible Church in 1988, in which I continue to serve as its senior pastor.

I mention all these details to point out that I know what I'm talking about when it comes to music. I believe I have earned respect in the field and can confidently say that I have the authority to engage myself on this issue.

In all the things I do as a minister of the gospel, I always want to be sure I can support my beliefs and practices with scriptural passages. I can confidently say that is also true with worship in music. My search has led me to the following verses. Ephesians 5:19–20 says, "Speaking to yourselves in psalms and hymns and spiritual songs, singing and making melody in your heart to the Lord; Giving thanks always for all things unto God and the Father in the name of our Lord Jesus Christ."

I find several truths from this passage that will help us organize the music in our churches:

I. Let us worship God together through music.

"Speaking to yourselves": Music is worshipping God in songs and instruments, using the appropriate elements. In musical worship, God's people commune together to worship God in total harmony. It is a symphonic approach of the people of God to praise and worship Him in unity. It is never a contest with worshippers out-singing each other or between instruments, with one trying to be more dominant than the others.

II. Let us worship God using the four different forms of music.

    A.   Psalms: these are scripture songs conveying the works and wondrous power of God as He dealt with Old Testament saints.

    B.   Hymns: these are songs of praise and adoration to God that declare His sovereignty and majesty.

    C.   Spiritual songs: these songs are testimonies about the work of the Holy Spirit in our lives and how He inspires and helps us overcome difficulties.

D. "Making melody in your heart": These are new songs God gave us to compose and perform for His glory. They show that God still inspires people to make wonderful music. Contemporary compositions with the right treatment are pleasing unto the Lord.

III. Let us always thank God in music.

"Giving thanks always": music is a great way to thank God for all His goodness.

This passage has inspired me to include all these forms of songs in church music. Incorporating these songs provides a good variety of ways to treat church music and, at the same time, show how He works in many different ways in the lives of believers. To have God-glorifying music in the church, the pastor or music director must have all the proper elements at play and all the biblical forms of music present in the music worship program.

A Sample Church Worship Program

1. Prelude: instrumental music
2. Opening song: hymn sung by the choir
3. Congregational hymn or medley of songs
4. Pastoral address or welcome
5. Welcoming of visitors
6. Welcoming song: new song for the month
7. Testimony
8. Choir: selected song
9. Offertory song: "Cheerful Giving"
10. Worship in giving: instrumental music
11. Special song
12. Bible pledge
13. Message
14. Invitation: spiritual or invitation song

15. Announcements
16. Closing song: "The Church with a Heart for Souls"

Music: The Mood Setter and Image Maker

People who work in music ministry must maintain a high standard in behavior and attire. Those who stand on the podium, such as choir members, must be appropriately dressed, such as coats for men and dresses for ladies. They must be in church ahead of everybody else to prepare for the opening song.

The worship team (composed of singers for different vocal parts) must be early to all services and be properly dressed or attired. The pianist and organist, together with the rest of the instrumentalists, must be in their positions before the start of the service.

Music provides a positive image for the church, so it is important for all participants in the music ministry to be organized and disciplined. The music director and song leader must always be prepared ahead of time to lead the congregational songs with the worship team and instrumentalists. He needs to plan the worship program a month in advance. A rehearsal must be scheduled to make the team feel comfortable to sing and lead. It is always important to project confidence in the pulpit.

Music is an excellent mood setter. Using appropriate songs and music in the church will help set the mood of the worshippers to worship and serve God. It is important that the pastor and the music director closely work together to choose the right music for the right message and occasion. As a universal language, music communicates excitement, love, grief, sadness, and other kinds of emotions that can affect the mood of listeners.

To have excellent and God-honoring music in a church, the music team must be well organized. It is composed of the following individuals:

1. Music director
2. Assistant music director or youth choir director

3. Children's choir director
4. Song leaders
5. Worship team (a singer from all vocal parts)
6. Instrumentalists (pianist, organist, orchestra)
7. Choir members (adult, youth, children)

Cheerful Giving

An Offertory Song
By Hernes M. Abante
September 10. 1998

I obey You, Lord, the Master of my soul,
Yielding my will to give my tithes and all,
Forsaking self to follow Your command
And obey You, Lord, and obey You, Lord.

I honor You, my King, my Deliverer,
For the cross You bore, Your blood, and eternal life.
Accept my gift to lift Your name up to the world.
With this increase, I honor You.

My loving Father, I thank You for the things You do,
The love You show, Your grace, and Your mercy too.
I offer You the firstfruits of my labors
To thank You, to thank You.

I worship You, my God. Oh Lord, I praise You.
I magnify Your name, express my love for You.
With my life and all I sacrifice for You,
I worship You, I worship You.

Stewardship of Giving

Giving is also an act of worship. It involves giving not only our tithes and offerings but also our lives to God. Coming to church is an act of giving. It is the giving of our time, our effort, and our attention to worship and glorify the Lord as a corporate body. It seeks to honor and praise God for all His goodness and grace.

The apostle Paul, in his writings in 2 Corinthians 8:1–7, described giving as an act of grace. It isn't an act of man's grace but of God's, signifying that to give is a privilege God gives to us. It is an opportunity for God to use us as a blessing to others. We aren't worthy to give anything to God, for there is nothing in us that can really give Him honor and glory. Besides, God owns all the things we give. We don't own anything in this world. He has only given us the privilege to give what He owns.

God wants us to give so He can bless us more. Giving is access to the unlimited resources of God. The Bible says in Luke 6:38, "Give, and it shall be given unto you; good measure, pressed down, and shaken together, and running over, shall men give into your bosom. For with the same measure that ye mete withal it shall be measured to you again."

If you want to receive, then give. What you receive will be commensurate with your gift. A believer who loves the Lord gives regularly and brings his or her gift to the storehouse, the church of Christ, the steward of God's promises.

Typically in the church, an opportunity to give is allowed when the offering plate is passed on to all the members during the offertory. Passing the offering plate, however, is a form of collecting, not giving. It presents an idea that the church is a collecting agency. This kind of giving not only presents an offensive stance to the people but also gives an impression that giving is forced, mandatory, and contrary to the spirit presented in the words the apostle Paul wrote in 2 Corinthians 9:7. "Every man according as he purposeth in his heart, so let him give; not grudgingly, or of necessity: for God loveth a cheerful giver."

For people to give cheerfully, the church must provide an atmosphere where they can give from the heart in a prayerful and worshipful manner. With this in place, giving becomes the work of the heart.

To provide the atmosphere of worship in giving, the International Bible Baptist Church doesn't pass offering plates. The people now come down to the altar and present their gifts personally before the man of God. They remain standing, praying, and worshipping God while presenting their gifts. This adjustment has noticeably changed the people's attitudes toward giving. They are silent, not talking, and they are communing with God. Giving becomes a true act of worship.

IBBC has adapted the principle of giving my brother, Dr. Benny M. Abante, the senior pastor of the Metropolitan Bible Baptist Church, conceptualized. He is currently serving in the House of Representatives as a congressman of the Sixth District of Manila, Philippines.

The "cheerful giving principle" isn't a new concept. It is the kind of giving taught and practiced in the first-century church. I encourage readers to apply the same principle in their congregations. Let me share with you the message of cheerful giving, which Dr. Benny Abante popularized:

I.   The Right Attitude in Giving

This refers to the attitude of the heart. Second Corinthians 9:7 says, "Every man according as he purposeth in his heart, so let him give; not grudgingly, or of necessity: for God loveth a cheerful giver."

A.   It means having a right relationship with God, and this relationship entails the giving of our lives.
B.   It means that giving is a decision of the heart; this is a giving of our lives and not just of our money.

1.   It is giving because it is right to give.
2.   It is giving even if nobody else gives.
3.   It is giving without expecting anything in return.

C.   It means giving unselfishly and unconditionally.
D.   It means giving faithfully and regularly.

II. The Four Levels of Motivations in Giving

The right motive in the cheerful giving principle refers to what makes you give or what moves you to give. Second Corinthians 8:8 says, "I speak not by commandment, but by occasion of the forwardness of others, and to prove the sincerity of your love."

People are motivated differently when it comes to giving. The saying "You can give without loving but you cannot love without giving" is true. Too often, giving is a selfish act, not always an act of love. What makes giving a blessing is when love is in it. Christians also give based on their level of maturity.

A. First level: giving as an answer to a command

2 Chronicles 31:5 says, "And as soon as the commandment came abroad, the children of Israel brought in abundance the firstfruits of corn, wine, and oil, and honey, and of all the increase of the field; and the tithe of all things brought they in abundantly."

1. This is the lowest level of giving.
2. It is the legalistic way to give.
3. It is giving the minimum.
4. It is the obedience of a fearful subject.

B. Second level: giving as an act to honor God

Proverbs 3:9–10 says, "Honour the LORD with thy substance, and with the firstfruits of all thine increase: So shall thy barns be filled with plenty, and thy presses shall burst out with new wine."

1. It is recognizing the goodness of God.
2. It is giving to God what He deserves.
3. In return, it is God recognizing His faithful steward.

C. Third level: giving as an act of thanksgiving

1. It is being a thankful child to his or her heavenly Father.
2. It isn't giving by constraint or force.

D. Fourth level: giving as an act of worship

1. It is an act of reverence of a subject to his or her Master.
2. It is an act of reverence of a faithful steward.
3. It is an act of reverence of a thankful son.
4. It is an act of reverence of an unworthy heir of God.

III. The Four Areas of Cheerful Giving

Right giving refers to the kind of gift according to the command of God. God has prescribed the kind of gift we ought to give. Do we give what we want to give, or do we give what God wants us to give? Second Chronicles 31:5 says, "And as soon as the commandment came abroad, the children of Israel brought in abundance the firstfruits of corn, wine, and oil, and honey, and of all the increase of the field; and the tithe of all things brought they in abundantly."

A. The tithes of all things

This is 10 percent of our gross income. It is the legal requirement in the Old Testament and the minimum standard of giving in the New Testament. Tithes take care of the house of God.

Malachi 3:10 says, "Bring ye all the tithes into the storehouse, that there may be meat in mine house, and prove me now herewith, saith the Lord of hosts, if I will not open you the windows of heaven, and pour you out a blessing, that there shall not be room enough to receive it."

B.   The increase

It is anything that is above our tithes. It is designed to support mission works outside the local church. In the New Testament, we believe in the grace of giving and not only in tithing (2 Cor. 8).

C.   The firstfruits

1.   It is a thanksgiving offering.

Deuteronomy 26:1–2 says, "And it shall be, when thou art come in unto the land which the Lord thy God giveth thee for an inheritance, and possessest it, and dwellest therein; That thou shalt take of the first of all the fruit of the earth, which thou shalt bring of thy land that the Lord thy God giveth thee, and shalt put it in a basket, and shalt go unto the place which the Lord thy God shall choose to place his name there."

2.   This is the best and sweetest of all regular offerings given annually.

Nehemiah 10:35 says, "And to bring the firstfruits of our ground, and the firstfruits of all fruit of all trees, year by year, unto the house of the Lord."

3.   The high priest, who ministers in the house of the Lord, is to use it. Deuteronomy 18:1–4 says,

The priests the Levites, and all the tribe of Levi, shall have no part nor inheritance with Israel: they shall eat the offerings of the Lord made by fire, and his inheritance. Therefore shall they have no inheritance among their brethren: the Lord is their inheritance, as he hath said unto them.

> And this shall be the priest's due from the people, from them that offer a sacrifice, whether it be ox or sheep; and they shall give unto the priest the shoulder, and the two cheeks, and the maw. The firstfruit also of thy corn, of thy wine, and of thine oil, and the first of the fleece of thy sheep, shalt thou give him.

4. It isn't to be delayed.
5. It should be laid at the apostles' feet.

Acts 4:35–37 says, "And laid them down at the apostles' feet: and distribution was made unto every man according as he had need. And Joses, who by the apostles was surnamed Barnabas, (which is, being interpreted, The son of consolation,) a Levite, and of the country of Cyprus, Having land, sold it, and brought the money, and laid it at the apostles' feet."

6. It is giving as God has prospered him, equivalent to at least one-month income.

First Corinthians 16:2 says, "Upon the first day of the week let every one of you lay by him in store, as God hath prospered him, that there be no gatherings when I come."

D. Sacrificial giving

> Also that day they offered great sacrifices, and rejoiced: for God had made them rejoice with great joy: the wives also and the children rejoiced: so that the joy of Jerusalem was heard even afar off. (Neh. 12:43)

> By him therefore let us offer the sacrifice of praise to God continually, that is, the fruit of our lips giving thanks to his name. (Heb. 13:15)

> Ye also, as lively stones, are built up a spiritual house, an holy priesthood, to offer up spiritual sacrifices, acceptable to God by Jesus Christ. (1 Peter 2:5)

IV. The Blessings in Relation to the Level of Giving

The blessings in giving go with the level of attitude. Giving is a heavenly investment that yields divine and eternal dividends. God is our Certified Perfect Accountant (CPA). As the Lord begins to bless, He also wants us to empty ourselves to Him—of sin and hindrances to take away the things that beset us so He might bless us even more.

> Wherefore seeing we also are compassed about with so great a cloud of witnesses, let us lay aside every weight, and the sin which doth so easily beset us, and let us run with patience the race that is set before us. (Heb. 12:1)

> Give, and it shall be given unto you; good measure, pressed down, and shaken together, and running over, shall men give into your bosom. For with the same measure that ye mete withal it shall be measured to you again. (Luke 6:38)

A.   "Good measure"

God is always honest with His people. We receive what we deserve—no more, no less. We reap what we sow. When we give the required minimum, our tithes, He blesses us in "good measure."

B.   "Pressed down"

God gives more than we give. We cannot out-give God. When we learn to give more than what we think we can afford, He blesses us more. He takes away some baggage in our lives to allow more blessings to come in.

C. "Shaken together"

God blesses more than we deserve. He takes away other hindrances and weights to allow blessings not only in one area of our lives but also in every area of our lives.

D. "Running over"

God has the joy in blessing us. His blessing is so overflowing that it cannot be contained. He continues to enlarge our reservoir and take away more hindrances to accommodate more blessings.

V. The Formula for Cheerful Giving.

First Corinthians 16:1–2 says, "Now concerning the collection for the saints, as I have given order to the churches of Galatia, even so do ye. Upon the first day of the week let every one of you lay by him in store, as God hath prospered him, that there be no gatherings when I come."

A. Giving must be regular: "upon the first day of the week."
B. Giving must be systematic: "Let every one of you lay by him in store."
C. Giving must be proportionate: "as God has prospered him."
D. Giving must be progressive: "he that soweth bountifully."

Second Corinthians 9:6 says, "But this I say, He which soweth sparingly shall reap also sparingly; and he which soweth bountifully shall reap also bountifully."

E. Giving must be with liberality: "abounded unto the riches of their liberality."

How that in a great trial of affliction the abundance of their joy and their deep poverty abounded unto the riches of their liberality. (2 Cor. 8:2)

For the administration of this service not only supplieth the want of the saints, but is abundant also by many thanksgivings unto God; Whiles by the experiment of this ministration they glorify God for your professed subjection unto the gospel of Christ, and for your liberal distribution unto them, and unto all men. (2 Cor. 9:12–13)

Practicing the cheerful giving principle teaches the people of God to trust in God's power and goodness. He can provide all the needs of the church. Many pastors and churches in the Philippines who have applied this principle are now able to provide for their building needs. It has also improved the financial status of the man of God through the giving of faithful stewards.

Chapter 11
CONCLUSION

Therefore as the church is subject unto Christ, so let the wives be to their own husbands in every thing. Husbands, love your wives, even as Christ also loved the church, and gave himself for it; That he might sanctify and cleanse it with the washing of water by the word, That he might present it to himself a glorious church, not having spot, or wrinkle, or any such thing; but that it should be holy and without blemish. So ought men to love their wives as their own bodies. He that loveth his wife loveth himself. For no man ever yet hated his own flesh; but nourisheth and cherisheth it, even as the Lord the church: For we are members of his body, of his flesh, and of his bones. For this cause shall a man leave his father and mother, and shall be joined unto his wife, and they two shall be one flesh. This is a great mystery: but I speak concerning Christ and the church. (Eph. 5:24–32)

When describing the relationship between the church and the Lord Jesus Christ, the apostle Paul paralleled it with the relationship between a wife and husband. The Lord showed us that the closest kind of relationship is a marital one. This is the most loving, most enduring relationship a man could ever experience.

The Lord yearns for this relationship. That's why He established the church. This dispensation of grace is a period of courtship and betrothal. He courts by winning people to Himself through redemption with a promise of eternal rewards. As soon as people receive Christ, they are encouraged to engage in fulfilling the relationship and fellowship through the local church, the betrothed bride of Christ. And in this betrothal period there is a period of faithfulness that must be proved and maintained until He comes. Faithfulness is tried and judged at the judgment seat of Christ, and those who are deemed "found faithful" (1 Corinthians 4:2) will be part of the bride in the marriage supper of the Lamb.

Church planting is seeking people for this eternal relationship. It is bringing people not only into a relationship with the Father but also to a closer and intimate fellowship with the Son. The faithful people of God, who constitute the church of God and the bride of Christ, will be presented unto Him as a glorious church.

The tasks of church planting and church building are serious ones with eternal blessings. Being chosen for this work should make us humble and, at the same time, proud that He has given us this privilege to be part of His glorious and heavenly plan.

To God be the glory. Great things he hath done! Revelation 21:9–27 says,

> And there came unto me one of the seven angels which had the seven vials full of the seven last plagues, and talked with me, saying, Come hither, I will shew thee the bride, the Lamb's wife. And he carried me away in the spirit to a great and high mountain, and shewed me that great city, the holy Jerusalem, descending out of heaven from God, Having the glory of God: and her light was like unto a stone most precious, even like a jasper stone, clear as crystal; And had a wall great and high, and had twelve gates, and at the gates twelve angels, and names written thereon, which are the names of the twelve tribes of the children of Israel: On the east three gates; on the north three gates; on the south three gates; and on the west three gates.
>
> And the wall of the city had twelve foundations, and in them the names of the twelve apostles of the Lamb. And he that

talked with me had a golden reed to measure the city, and the gates thereof, and the wall thereof.

And the city lieth foursquare, and the length is as large as the breadth: and he measured the city with the reed, twelve thousand furlongs. The length and the breadth and the height of it are equal. And he measured the wall thereof, an hundred and forty and four cubits, according to the measure of a man, that is, of the angel. And the building of the wall of it was of jasper: and the city was pure gold, like unto clear glass. And the foundations of the wall of the city were garnished with all manner of precious stones. The first foundation was jasper; the second, sapphire; the third, a chalcedony; the fourth, an emerald; The fifth, sardonyx; the sixth, sardius; the seventh, chrysolite; the eighth, beryl; the ninth, a topaz; the tenth, a chrysoprasus; the eleventh, a jacinth; the twelfth, an amethyst.

And the twelve gates were twelve pearls; every several gate was of one pearl: and the street of the city was pure gold, as it were transparent glass.

And I saw no temple therein: for the Lord God Almighty and the Lamb are the temple of it. And the city had no need of the sun, neither of the moon, to shine in it: for the glory of God did lighten it, and the Lamb is the light thereof. And the nations of them which are saved shall walk in the light of it: and the kings of the earth do bring their glory and honour into it. And the gates of it shall not be shut at all by day: for there shall be no night there. And they shall bring the glory and honour of the nations into it. And there shall in no wise enter into it any thing that defileth, neither whatsoever worketh abomination, or maketh a lie: but they which are written in the Lamb's book of life.

Thanksgiving Song

By Hernes M. Abante
November 27, 1998

I thank You, my God,
For the things You have done to me:
Your goodness each day,
For loving me richly.
Thank You for Your grace
That opens heaven's golden door.
Oh my God,
I thank You.

Chorus:

From my heart, I sing You this song.
Humbly I yield to Your loving call.
My only desire is to give You praise.
Thank You, Lord. I thank You, Lord.

Your goodness, Lord, is great.
Your mercy's full of tenderness.
Your great faithfulness
Secures my eternity.
Thank You for Your love
That hides my unworthiness.
My precious God,
I thank You.

Printed in the United States
By Bookmasters